How to Lead It: Primary Art and Design

Naomi Pilling
Series editor: Jon Hutchinson

BLOOMSBURY EDUCATION
LONDON OXFORD NEW YORK NEW DELHI SYDNEY

BLOOMSBURY EDUCATION
Bloomsbury Publishing Plc
50 Bedford Square, London WC1B 3DP, UK
Bloomsbury Publishing Ireland Limited
29 Earlsfort Terrace, Dublin 2, D02 AY28, Ireland

BLOOMSBURY, BLOOMSBURY EDUCATION and the
Diana logo are trademarks of Bloomsbury Publishing Plc

First published in Great Britain, 2026 by Bloomsbury Publishing Plc

This edition published in Great Britain, 2026 by Bloomsbury Publishing Plc

A catalogue record for this book is available from the British Library

ISBN: PB: 978-1-80199-832-1; ePub: 978-1-80199-830-7

2 4 6 8 10 9 7 5 3 1 (paperback)

Cover design by Sophie Gordon

Typeset by Lumina Datamatics Ltd
Printed and bound in Great Britain by TJ Books, Padstow, Cornwall

FSC www.fsc.org MIX Paper | Supporting responsible forestry FSC® C013056

To find out more about our authors and books visit www.bloomsbury.com
and sign up for our newsletters

For product safety related questions contact productsafety@bloomsbury.com

Contents

Acknowledgements

I would like to thank my editor, Grace Kelly, for her hard work and her calm, objective voice in helping to put this book together. Also, thank you to my inspirational colleagues at the Primary Knowledge Curriculum, without whom I would not have been in the position to write this book. Finally, thanks to my unfailingly loyal husband, Ben, who has read every word, and provided his thoughts and insights. This book is in memory of my mum, a passionate primary school teacher, who believed in, and taught me, the power and importance of creativity.

1 Leading art and design

Leading art and design in a primary school is an exciting role. Art allows pupils to explore and develop visual, perceptual and creative capabilities in a way which no other discipline offers. A good art education in a primary school offers pupils a rich blend of learning about the *language* of art and the opportunity to develop the skills and processes to *create* art.

You may feel that taking on the role of a leader for art and design perfectly suits your own interest and expertise in the visual arts. For many people however, it is a subject in which they lack confidence. Maybe you feel unsure about your knowledge and skills or it is your first experience in leading a subject. Whichever applies to you, this book is designed to be a practical guide to help you ensure an excellent provision and experience for every pupil in your school.

When I first qualified as a primary school teacher I was passionate about introducing pupils to the rich and varied world of art. Giving them the opportunity to express and develop their own creativity was something to which I aspired. I soon found that realising this aspiration in my own Year 3 classroom, at a time when the pressures of achieving results in English and maths seemed paramount, was a more remote possibility than I had hoped. Ten years on, I want to impart what I have learned, and what I wish I had known in my early days as a teacher.

This chapter looks at:

- the aims of an art and design education in primary school
- the role of a primary art and design leader
- current challenges in teaching the subject
- opportunities to overcome educational challenges in art and design provision
- how this book can support you in your art and design leadership role.

Aims of primary art and design education

What is art and design in the primary context and what are the aims of a high-quality art and design education?

The current National Curriculum for England (DfE, 2013) sets out how art and design is a blend of:

- Acquiring knowledge and skills to be able to *create* art, craft and design and in doing so developing creative, imaginative and reflective capabilities.
- Developing the ability to think critically and *learn about* art, craft and design from a variety of cultures, thinking about how it can reflect and influence society.

The National Curriculum refers to art, craft and design. In Chapter 3 we will explore the distinctions and overlap between these three definitions and what this means in relation to curriculum content. The rest of this chapter uses the term 'art' to refer to all three areas.

Ofsted's research review series: art and design (2023) echoes how the National Curriculum identifies the dual nature of art in schools (*creating* art and *learning about* art) with the following summary: 'a high-quality art education can build pupils' ability to appreciate and interpret what they observe, communicate what they feel, or make what they imagine and invent. At its best, the subject is both intellectually challenging and creatively demanding' (Ofsted, 2023). Pupils learn by making connections between encountering art by others, and the art which they create themselves.

Rather than an exercise in ticking off a series of skills acquired, concepts learned and names or dates memorised, learning in art goes much deeper. In this subject, the process of looking at, talking about and making art can provide a pupil with an understanding of how art can enrich their inner world and provide a vehicle for expression and identity. As such, it has the potential to unlock life-long interest and pleasure. High-quality education in art is also essential for the creative industries, which are currently central to our economy.

Creativity

Because a large part of the discipline of art is about *making* art, debate about what should be in a good art education often focuses on the concept of 'creativity'. The English National Curriculum says that pupils should produce work using materials 'creatively'. What is creativity and how can we define it? The word is often used in a casual, non-specific way, which can be unhelpful for teachers when considering what we should teach, how to teach it and how to assess it.

Creativity has been described as the 'capacity to imagine, conceive, express, or make something that was not there before' (NACCCE, 1999). Defining it in this way captures how creativity is bound up with the idea of self-expression. This is sometimes seen as being in conflict with learning techniques or skills, or what we might categorise as formal art instruction (APPG, 2023).

This tension is illustrated by the National Society of Education in Art and Design's (NSEAD) response to Ofsted's research review (2023). The Ofsted review suggests that pupils need to learn specific knowledge before they can express their creative capacity in what they make. For example, on drawing, the review says: 'Once pupils have learned the components of drawing, they can gain further knowledge and explore creative possibilities' (Ofsted, 2023).

In their response to the review NSEAD says that this approach, with creativity coming at a later point after learning particular skills, is too linear. They say that this view 'does not give value to expression, experimentation, invention or communication' (NSEAD, 2023). Having taught art for many years I tend to agree: creative exploration can occur and should be encouraged at every stage of learning. It is more organic and fluid than perhaps the research review suggests. Creative development and the development of skills may, in fact, occur concurrently. A Reception pupil, for example, may learn that there are three special colours called the primary colours through painting an imaginary creature using blue, yellow and red.

The research review emphasises the need to learn certain skills and techniques before exploring how to use these creatively. This may be to guard against approaches which try to foster the creative process in a vacuum of knowledge. A good curriculum needs to provide opportunity for practising different skills and techniques (e.g. different ways of creating tone with a pencil by way of shading or cross-hatching) which a pupil can develop using their own creative style and imagination. Practising a particular technique so that it is performed with a degree of automaticity and fluidity (for example, shading with a pencil) allows a pupil expressive freedom in how they use, or choose not to use, a particular technique. The balance between creative exploration and learning skills and techniques is discussed further in Chapter 8.

A final note on creativity: it is good to provide opportunities for pupils to express themselves but we don't want to restrict their art experiences to only self-expression and novelty. There are some artistic disciplines that require extensive practice and the ability to follow established conventions very closely, such as some Islamic art and traditional Chinese brush painting. It is good to give pupils exposure to these sorts of disciplines too.

The role of a primary art and design leader

As primary art and design leaders we need to make sure that there is a clear plan about what pupils are going to learn in their art lessons and ensure that they are learning effectively. This means having a specified curriculum, and monitoring and reviewing its implementation. We should aspire to promote the subject, allowing pupils in our schools to discover the rich cultural and creative opportunities it provides.

We can break down what this means for subject leaders into six areas.

1. Curriculum development

Subject leads should:

- Have an overall vision of the aims and purposes of the art and design curriculum.
- Oversee and work with teachers to develop a rich, balanced curriculum which incorporates both a breadth and depth of knowledge.
- Develop a long-term plan which details how pupils' knowledge and skills will progress from year to year.
- Ensure the curriculum is inclusive and has high expectations for all pupils including those with special educational needs and disabilities (SEND) and English as an additional language (EAL).
- Oversee consistent curriculum implementation including ensuring appropriate timetable allocation.
- Develop appropriate systems which monitor pupils' overall progress and curriculum effectiveness.
- Implement appropriate modifications as a result of monitoring.

2. Resourcing

Planning and acquiring resources for your subject will involve:

- Managing resources in line with budget and curriculum requirements.
- Ordering, allocating and storing resources.
- Auditing resources on a regular basis.
- Ensuring all risk assessment and health and safety requirements are met.

3. Monitoring teaching and learning

Ensuring successful implementation of the curriculum is known as monitoring. We can think of this as gathering evidence, reviewing and improving. This includes:

- Regularly reviewing planning.
- Observing lessons.
- Undertaking informal learning walks.
- Looking at and discussing sketchbooks/outcomes with pupils.
- Undertaking pupil voice.
- Giving feedback to teachers/discussing findings with SLT.
- Implementing modifications to improve.

4. Supporting colleagues

You can foster a supportive working environment by:

- Encouraging regular subject updates in staff meetings.
- Ensuring teachers understand what is going well in art lessons and give clear, achievable targets from lesson observations.
- Agreeing a clear strategy for the best use of support staff in art lessons.
- Making time to plan together.
- Creating the opportunity for peer-on-peer lesson observations.
- Providing staff training in areas pinpointed for development.

5. Raising the profile of art and design

Art and design in a school is not just about lessons. Promoting it as a subject could include:

- Running art clubs.
- Arranging class trips to galleries and museums.
- Investigating and using parental expertise, e.g. Class talks/demonstrations.
- Investigating local opportunities for visiting artists/workshops.

- Participating in gallery/museum projects/competitions.
- Creating displays to celebrate pupils' work.
- Having a yearly whole-school art event.
- Using technology to showcase pupils' work to a wider audience.

6. Professional development

As subject leads it is important that we are supported in our leadership role so that we make the best of it, which in turn will help us to provide the best art and design education for children in our schools. Developing our own knowledge can include:

- Attending courses/training delivered by museums/galleries, subject organisations or advisers/consultants.
- Sharing expertise with other art leaders in other schools from the local area, multi-academy trust or federation.
- Keeping up to date with the latest, subject specific educational research.

Finding focus and prioritising

The list of responsibilities above can seem overwhelming at first. It is important to realise that we can't focus on everything at once. We need to decide each academic year what our priorities are and make a realistic, time-specified plan. A good method is to create a subject development plan in the first half of the Autumn term each year, which can be reviewed throughout the course of the year. A suggested format using the focus areas set out previously is provided in the following table.

If art is a subject which has been neglected in your school before you took on your leadership role, the focus may be devising and implementing a new curriculum in the first half of the year, with regular milestones for monitoring how it is going. In contrast, in a school where art is a well-established subject the focus may be on keeping a regular check on how the curriculum is being implemented, addressing any issues which are highlighted by monitoring and focusing on profile/enrichment.

Action	Responsibility	Timescale/resources	Progress
Curriculum development			
Resources			
Monitoring teaching and learning			
Supporting colleagues			
Raising the profile			
Professional development			

Current educational challenges

The general picture

Despite the benefits of a high-quality education in art and design, reports on its position in schools over the last decade paint a bleak picture.

- The Fabian Society report on the arts in general stated that 'there has been a dramatic decline in both the quantity and quality of arts education in primary schools in England' (Cooper, 2018).
- By 2023 The Arts in Schools report found 'a lack of value ascribed to the arts within the state education system in England' (Bacon and Tambling, 2023).
- In 2024 the Cultural Learning Alliance reported that numbers of arts GCSEs taken had fallen by 42 per cent since 2010 and there were 14 per cent fewer arts teachers in schools than there were in 2010 (CLA, 2024).
- In a recent survey 76 per cent of teachers agreed that art education is not prioritised in schools (Art-K, 2025).

A summary of the challenges

Various surveys of teachers and pupils show significant challenges in providing a high-quality art and design education at school level. These include the following.

Teacher knowledge, confidence and training:

- **Primary teachers' lack of confidence teaching art and design**. A lack of understanding of the subject leads to fewer art lessons and a narrower range of experiences offered to pupils (APPG, 2023).
- **A deficit of training in initial teacher training**. Trainee primary teachers receive between three to12 hours of training to teach art and design (APPG, 2023).
- **A lack of subject-specific training in art and design.** Around 21 per cent of primary teachers say they had never attended any subject-specific training since their initial teacher training. (APPG, 2023).

Workforce and teacher morale:

- As many as 68.6 per cent of primary art leaders have considered **leaving the profession** (APPG, 2023).
- For teachers teaching art and design, 86.4 per cent said their **workload had increased** in the last five years (APPG, 2023).

Decrease in financial resources:

- **A lack of money for resources**. Around 93.2 per cent of teachers say that there has been a decrease in resources since the Covid pandemic (APPG, 2023).
- **A decline in extra-curricular provision** since the Covid pandemic. Schools report cutting 50 per cent of trips and outings for financial reasons (APPG, 2023).

Lesson time:

- It's reported that 18 per cent of primary teachers spend **no time at all teaching art in an average week** (Art-K, 2025).

Decrease in fine motor skills:

- Around 77 per cent of teachers have witnessed a **worsening in pupils' ability to perform precise movements** such as holding a pencil, drawing, writing or using scissors since 2020 (Art-K, 2025).

Racial and social inequities:

- In 2025 the Cultural Learning Alliance reported that there is a **clear relationship between the poverty of an area and pupils in that area not studying the expressive arts in school**. Expressive arts take-up at GCSE and A Level is lowest where there is the highest level of free school meals and levels of deprivation (CLA, 2025).
- The Education Policy Institute highlights that **children in independent schools are much more likely to attend extra-curricular arts activities than children from state schools.** Students who are eligible for free school meals are also much less likely than their peers who are not eligible for free school meals to attend arts activities (CLA, 2025).
- The Sutton Trust reported that young adults from working-class backgrounds are **four times less likely to work in the creative industries compared to their middle-class peers** (CLA, 2025).

Opportunities to overcome the educational challenges

All this paints a rather bleak picture for art and design in schools. However, my own experience of working with subject leads in schools in recent years suggests a more hopeful perspective.

In primary schools, art is a compulsory subject in all four national curricula of the UK and plays a significant part in the life of lots of schools. Since the introduction of the Ofsted inspection framework in 2019, there has been more emphasis placed on the teaching and inspection of discrete subjects. As a result, in recent years primary schools have been more motivated to ensure arts subjects are treated seriously and appropriate hours are allotted within the primary timetable. Whilst there is still a battle in Year 6 to persuade primary schools not to drop subjects that are not examined by Key Stage 2 SATs, Ofsted's emphasis on focusing on the successful implementation of a coherent and well-sequenced curriculum seems to have had a positive effect.

The decline of the arts in schools has motivated interested individuals and arts organisations to advocate and campaign for their resurgence. At the same time, they have provided opportunities and resources, many of which are referred to in this book. The Ofsted research review series: art and design (2023) raised the profile of the importance of art in schools and provided clarity about curriculum content, pedagogy and assessment. This is invaluable for subject leads.

If we are passionate about the benefits of art in schools, it can provide motivation to make a difference in our own particular setting. It is within our power as subject leads to do that. I have seen many schools where subject leads have made art central in their schools by driving the successful implementation of a well-sequenced, balanced curriculum that allows all pupils to thrive. This book aims to help you do just that.

How this book can support you

This book offers practical support for subject leaders with limited time. You may like to dip into chapters/parts of chapters out of order, where you have identified a particular area where you need support.

Throughout the book you will find:

- examples to illustrate best practice
- advice about teaching different skills/technique
- case studies for further exemplification
- suggestions for staff professional development
- reflection questions
- follow-up reading and suggested resources.

The next chapter discusses how we can get the best from research evidence. Chapters 3–5 look at principles of curriculum design, planning a curriculum and what makes an effective lesson.

Chapter 6 discusses the importance of looking and visual literacy in art lessons. Chapter 7 considers how to guide practice through modelling/demonstration and scaffolding and Chapter 8 discusses practice and the importance of process. Chapter 9 looks at basic principles in drawing, painting and sculpture and discusses key resources in relation to each area. Chapter 10 discusses assessment, monitoring and how to implement change.

Chapter summary

- Learning art at primary school includes acquiring knowledge and skills to be able to *create* art and developing the ability to think critically and *learn about* art from a variety of cultures.
- A good curriculum should provide opportunity for practising different skills and techniques, which a pupil can develop using their own creative style and imagination.
- As primary art and design leaders we need to ensure there is a specified curriculum, and monitor and review its implementation.
- Significant educational challenges exist in art education, which include teacher knowledge, confidence and training, a lack of funding, a lack of emphasis and importance placed on the subject and social and racial inequities.
- Despite the challenges, subject leads have an opportunity to make a significant difference in schools, promoting art and design to allow all pupils to discover the rich cultural and creative opportunities which it provides.

Questions for reflection

- What is the profile of art in my school?
- How much art is there in the timetable?
- What is the level of teacher confidence in teaching art?
- Do the pupils both *make* art and *learn about* art?
- How are they being given the opportunity to develop their creative and expressive capabilities?

Explore further

- 'Art Now: An Inquiry into the State of Art and Design teaching in Early Years Foundation Stage, Primary and Secondary Education' (2023), by APPG (All-Party Parliamentary Group for Art, Craft and Design in Education): www.nsead.org/files/13a555d0c7a3c66da64bfb8049a4dae1.pdf

- 'Research review series: art and design' (2023) by Ofsted: www.gov.uk/government/publications/research-review-series-art-and-design
- Cultural Learning Alliance who are a source of arts education news and lead a cross-arts agenda for arts/cultural learning policy change: www.culturallearningalliance.org.uk
- NSEAD (National Society for Education in Art and Design) which issues resources and various publications containing recent research: www.nsead.org

2 Getting the best from research evidence

Research evidence about teaching and schools can be a useful tool to help teachers and leaders refine and improve their practice. Using research evidence to guide practice means understanding the significance and reliability of findings and interpreting how these can be usefully used in the classroom. We need to remember that not all the research we come across will fit with our unique school context.

As a subject lead we need to know how to find relevant research evidence, how to interpret it and what use we can make of it in the context of teaching art and design. This involves taking a thoughtful approach, questioning the implications for a study and adapting its insights in ways that reflect the needs, priorities and realities of the pupils, staff and curriculum goals.

In this chapter we will think about:

- what is research evidence?
- guiding principles for interpreting research evidence
- sources of research evidence and discussion
- key findings from cognitive science
- Rosenshine's principles.

What is research evidence?

Research evidence is not the same as general sources of information about education. It is described as 'evidence generated through planned and systematic processes that answer specific questions, often assessing the impact of practices or approaches' (EEF, 2024). This is different from individual school-based data.

Other sources, which are not research evidence, such as articles, blogs, podcasts, etc. are likely to be useful to teachers and schools in providing opinion and discussion. Where they make claims on the basis of research, we must always trace that evidence back to its source to assess its reliability. Publication, in whatever form, is not in and of itself an indicator of authority.

There are different categories of research evidence. These are summarised in the EEF's 'Using research evidence: a concise guide' (2024). Gathering a range of research evidence can be useful, but quantitative studies which measure cause and effect are more likely to be useful for understanding impact/effectiveness.

Guiding principles for interpreting research evidence

'Using research evidence: a concise guide' (EEF, 2024) provides a useful guide to interpreting research evidence. It sets out guidelines and questions to ask to be able to assess the reliability of evidence. These can be summarised as:

- **What is the sample?** Consider the sample size: large scale studies are generally more reliable. Ask if the sample is representative of pupils generally and if the study records limitations or restrictions in the sample(s) used.
- **What methods are used?** Consider if the methods of the study are explained clearly. Ask if the data collected/analysed is appropriate and relevant to the question posed by the study.
- **Is the evidence independent?** Consider if there is any author/organisation that has a personal stake in the study which could affect the credibility of its findings. Ask if the study has been shared or published commercially and if so why.
- **Are conclusions supported?** Consider whether the study reports only some or all of its findings. Ask if the conclusion seems one-sided.
- **Is the evidence applicable?** Consider whether findings have been extended to situations or people the research wasn't intended for. Ask if the research can be applied in a real-life classroom context.

Sources: evidence and discussion

There is a relatively small amount of specialist research evidence about teaching art and design (Gregory et al., 2020). The Ofsted research review (2023) offers a useful summary of existing research and is a good place to start reading to understand developments over the last 20 years. Let's consider where to look for research evidence, discussion/opinion about teaching the arts generally and research specific to art and design.

Organisations

The Education Endowment Foundation (EEF) is a charity that aims to support schools to improve teaching and learning through better use of evidence-based research. It was set up to improve attainment of pupils from lower socio-economic backgrounds. It produces guidance reports, carries out its own research into the implementation of specific strategies and runs programs in schools.

The Chartered College of Teaching is a professional body for teachers. It provides professional development training, carries out research and produces publications which focus on the development of evidence-informed practice.

The Cultural Learning Alliance (CLA) is a charity which campaigns for an arts-rich education for all children. It gathers and collates evidence and produces reports and commentary about the benefit of the arts for young people.

The National Society for Education in Art and Design (NSEAD) is the society, trade union and professional organisation for art, craft and design educators in the UK. It provides resources, professional development training, commentary and research. It publishes a blog, a magazine and an international journal.

Publications, blogs and podcasts

Impact is a termly journal produced by The Chartered College of Teaching containing peer-reviewed articles connecting research findings with classroom practice.

The International Journal of Art and Design Education (iJADE) is an international journal produced by NSEAD which includes articles about theoretical and practical approaches in art and design education in all sectors.

AD Magazine is a magazine for UK based art, craft and design educators produced by NSEAD.

Thinking Deeply About Primary Education is a podcast focusing solely on the primary sector, interviewing primary teachers, leaders and subject specialists.

The Evidence Based Education Podcast is a podcast about evidence-based practices, impact and outcomes.

Mind the Gap is a podcast debating best practice in the classroom, research-based approaches and sustaining effective professional development.

Key findings from cognitive science

The growing field of cognitive science offers research evidence about how our brains work. This comes from two main areas of study: neuroscience and psychology. The field of cognitive science includes research and understanding about how we learn and, as such, has become foundational for teachers and schools. Reflection on key findings from cognitive science is important for any subject lead to ensure effective teaching of their subject.

Learning has been described as 'a change in long-term memory' (Kirschner et al., 2006). One of the key insights from cognitive science, the theoretical model of working memory (Baddeley and Hitch, 1974), helps us to understand what this means. The model has been explained by the cognitive psychologist Daniel Willingham (2009). It describes the mind as consisting of two parts: working memory and long-term memory. Working memory is the site of our conscious thinking where information is processed. It has limited capacity. It is thought that an average person can hold about four pieces of information in the working memory (Cowan, 2010). If information is encoded (or processed) it enters the long-term memory, which has a virtually limitless capacity. This is learning. Information in the long-term memory can be remembered or retrieved back into the working memory. Retrieval needs to happen multiple times otherwise it is likely that the information will be forgotten.

The model of working memory and related ideas and findings from cognitive science have implications for how we teach. Some of these are summarised in the EEF's *Cognitive Science Approaches in the Classroom: A Review of the Evidence* (2021) and are explored below.

In practice: key ideas from cognitive science and implementation in the art classroom

The following table analyses some key ideas from cognitive science as set out in the EEF's *Cognitive Science Approaches in the Classroom: A Review of the Evidence* (2021) and considers their implications in the art classroom.

Key ideas from cognitive science	Implications in the art classroom
Spaced learning • This means spacing teaching and learning of material over time. Pupils revisit a specific concept, idea or skill several times over the course of one week, or once or twice a week for many weeks. It is often combined with retrieval practice. • When pupils revisit knowledge in this way, when it is almost forgotten, it increases the likelihood of knowledge being embedded in pupils' long-term memory. • This is in contrast to concentrated and uninterrupted blocked study or practice, over a short period. • More studies have examined the impact of spacing content across days rather than within lessons.	• This has implications for curriculum design discussed in Chapters 3 and 4. • Rather than teaching art in a block, for example, for a whole day once every half-term, it is better to teach one lesson each week. • Revisiting content in a weekly art lesson increases the likelihood of knowledge being embedded in the pupils' long-term memory. • For example, over a course of six weekly lessons, Year 1 pupils learn about primary colours, mixing secondary colours and use primary and secondary colours to paint a variety of images.

Retrieval practice
• This is the process of recalling information from the long-term memory with little or minimal prompting.
• It requires pupils to think hard to recall the information they have retained.
• It is thought that retrieval practice encourages pupils to strengthen their memory of key concepts.
• Retrieval practice is in contrast to a teacher reminding pupils about previous learning.
	• This has implications for the content and structure of a lesson, as discussed in Chapter 5.
	• Retrieval practice can be successfully used at the beginning of an art lesson, so that pupils can build on what they already know.
	• A plenary at the end of a lesson or at various points during a lesson can also give pupils the opportunity to retrieve aspects of what they have learned.
	• As well as activating prior knowledge, retrieval practice allows teachers to assess what pupils know and remember, and address any gaps in knowledge or misconceptions which may have arisen.
	• Some successful techniques for retrieval include:
	  ◦ using multiple choice questions
	  ◦ short-answer fact questions
	  ◦ true/false questions
	  ◦ image recognition
	  ◦ recitation of definitions.

Managing cognitive load
• Learning can be hindered if the demands on working memory are too great.
• This can occur if pupils are faced with too much new information simultaneously. This can be exacerbated where a pupil has limited prior knowledge in their long-term memory to draw on.
• Activating prior knowledge can reduce extraneous cognitive load on the working memory so pupils can focus on new material.
	• This has implications for how to teach an art lesson, discussed in more detail in Chapters 5 and 7.
	• Cognitive load can be managed by:
	  ◦ presenting new material, such as the practice of a new technique (for example, working from dark to light with acrylics) in small steps
	  ◦ providing models, such as a worked example of a particular technique (for example, cross-hatching)
	  ◦ providing scaffolds, such as sentence stems or physical scaffolds (for example, a pencil grip).

Working with schemas • Schemas are structures that organise knowledge in the mind. The mind connects new information with pre-existing knowledge, developing existing schemas. • New knowledge must fit in with what is already known/understood. Pupils use existing knowledge to make use of new content. • The more interconnected our existing knowledge structures are, the more efficiently we can make sense of and organise new information.	• This has implications for curriculum design and sequencing, discussed in Chapters 3 and 4. • An art curriculum should allow pupils to learn practical, theoretical and disciplinary knowledge and make connections between these three areas. • This means designing a curriculum where knowledge and skills build year on year. • This requires specifying and planning in each lesson, unit and for each year group what practical, theoretical and disciplinary knowledge a pupil will learn, making sure that it connects with what they have previously learned.

Multimedia learning
• This refers to the practice of using more than one medium to teach, such as visual and audio materials.
• It is based on the idea that working memory has two distinct parts, one that deals with visual and spatial information and the other that deals with auditory information.
• By presenting content in multiple formats, teachers can activate both parts of the working memory to aid learning.
	• This idea emphasises the importance of looking at and discussing art, discussed in detail in Chapter 6.
	• It also has implications for other aspects about how to teach an art lesson, discussed in more detail in Chapters 5 and 7. This includes:
	  ◦ introducing new vocabulary with simple corresponding pictures
	  ◦ presenting simple pictures alongside written or spoken explanations.

Embodied learning and physical factors	

• This refers to strategies that engage and make use of movement and the body to aid learning.
• It is thought that teachers may be able to make new information more easily comprehensible and memorable by engaging physical movement.
	• This idea emphasises the importance of the practical act of making art, discussed in detail in Chapters 7, 8 and 9.
	• It also has implications for other aspects about how to teach an art lesson, discussed in more detail in Chapters 5 and 7. This includes:
	  • introducing new vocabulary with simple corresponding actions
	  • rehearsing physical actions as a precursor to using materials, such as drawing a line or shape in the air with a finger, before using a pencil.

Rosenshine's principles

Much of what cognitive science has shown us about how pupils learn are reflected in Rosenshine's principles (2012). These are ten research-based principles of instruction based on a long period of research which looked at what effective teachers do. The research considered cognitive science, classroom practices and cognitive support (procedures which support learning and memory).

The ten principles are a helpful summary of ideas which can provide a focus for subject leads when assessing what is working, and what is not, in the art classroom. They can be split into three overarching categories: retrieval, explicit teaching and practice. The table sets out the principles with a short summary of how these relate to ideas from cognitive science, explained earlier in this chapter. It indicates where you can find more about these principles in the context of teaching art in the following chapters.

Retrieval See Chapters 5 and 7	Explicit teaching See Chapters 5 and 7	Practice See Chapter 7
• Begin a lesson with a short review of previous learning. • Engage students in a weekly and monthly review. • See 'Retrieval practice' on page 17.	• Present new material in small steps. • Provide models. • Provide scaffolds. • See 'Managing cognitive load' on page 18.	• Guide student practice. • Require and monitor independent practice. • Obtain a high success rate. • See 'Managing cognitive load', 'Multimedia learning' and 'Embodied learning' on pages 18 and 19.
• Check for understanding throughout. • Ask lots of questions. • See Chapter 5 for more detail.		

Example PD session: using multimedia and embodied learning in the classroom

Here is an example of a PD session where teachers can think about how to use multimedia and embodied teaching techniques to aid learning in the art classroom.

TIMING SUGGESTION	SESSION GUIDANCE
20 mins	• Read the EEF's guidance in 'Cognitive Science Approaches in the Classroom: A Review of the Evidence' (2021) about (1) multimedia and (2) embodied learning. • In pairs, review the material together and make a list of ten important points summarising each of the two sections. • Explain that the teachers will use their understanding about multimedia and embodied learning to help plan their next art lesson.

30 mins	Instruct teachers to choose an art lesson they are about to teach and ask them to:
	
	• Consider what corresponding pictures/actions they will use to teach vocabulary.
	• Consider what simple pictures they can use alongside written or spoken explanations.
	• How they might introduce pupils to a piece of art they will encounter during the lesson, for example:
	  • Ask pupils to imagine they have jumped into the picture and are walking around in it. Ask them to think about what they can *see* and how they *feel*.
	  • Ask pupils to 're-enact' the image using their bodies and objects in the room.
	  • Ask pupils to 'draw' the image in the air with their finger.
	  • Ask pupils to draw the image from their partner's description.
	  • Create a reproduction of the image and cut it up into pieces so it resembles a jigsaw puzzle. In groups, ask pupils to put the jigsaw together.
	• Discuss what physical actions they can rehearse with the pupils to aid their use of materials during the lesson.

10 mins	Feedback, review and reflect on the planning the teachers have done as a group.

Chapter summary

- Research evidence about teaching and schools can be useful to help teachers and leaders refine and improve their practice.
- Research evidence is generated through planned and systematic processes.
- We can use a series of questions to review the reliability of research evidence.
- The theoretical model of working memory helps us understand how pupils learn.
- We can use key findings from cognitive science (such as spaced practice, working with schemas, retrieval practice, managing cognitive load, multimedia learning and embodied learning) to inform good practice in the art classroom.
- Much of what cognitive science has shown us about how pupils learn are reflected in Rosenshine's principles.

Questions for reflection

- Reflect on your own knowledge of cognitive science and principles which apply to teaching art. Which one or two of the sources/publications above could you read/listen to, to improve your understanding?
- Consider what teachers in your school understand about cognitive science. Is there one area from the table on pages 17–19 ('key ideas from cognitive science and implementation in the art classroom') which could be the basis of a staff meeting to improve the teaching of art in your school?
- Consider Rosenshine's principles. How could you make use of these with the teachers in your school to improve the teaching of art?

Explore further

- EEF's guide for using research evidence (2024): https://d2tic4wvo1iusb.cloudfront.net/production/documents/using_research_evidence_-_a_concise_guide.pdf?v=1769250511
- EEF's guide about cognitive science (2021):

  https://d2tic4wvo1iusb.cloudfront.net/production/documents/guidance/Cognitive_science_approaches_in_the_classroom_-_A_review_of_the_evidence.pdf?v=1769163226
- Barak Rosenshine's article 'Principles of Instruction' (2012): www.aft.org/sites/default/files/Rosenshine.pdf
- NSEAD's website: www.nsead.org
- Ofsted's Research Review Series for Art and Design (2023): www.gov.uk/government/publications/research-review-series-art-and-design#

3 Curriculum planning principles

There is no single way to plan a curriculum. Some schools might plan it themselves, some may use a variety of sources and other schools may use schemes from external providers. Similarly, no two primary art curricula will look completely alike. Part of the joy of art and design is that it is a diverse and developing discipline. The artists, art and methods that pupils learn about may vary considerably between different schools.

Despite this diversity there are overarching principles which can help us ensure that the curriculum we devise or use is effective. These principles consider what pupils should learn, how knowledge and skills develop over time, and how learning is sequenced to build confidence and creativity. For art and design leaders this means zooming out and thinking about progression and coherence across the whole school. At the same time, curriculum planning must remain responsive to the unique context of the school, including the people, staff expertise, resources and community.

This chapter guides you through some of these principles to help you shape a curriculum that is both ambitious and inclusive of all pupils.

We will consider:

- what is a curriculum?
- art and design as a discipline
- knowledge in art
- making curriculum choices: breadth and depth
- specification and sequencing
- ambition and inclusivity.

What is a curriculum?

Put simply, a curriculum is what we intend to teach. It should outline, with specificity, what we teach and when we teach it. If it is coherently designed, it should allow pupils' knowledge and skills to grow, so that the teacher in one year group can pick up where the last teacher left off.

This makes it sound simple. The very concept and definition of curriculum, however, is seen by experts as immensely complicated. Deciding what should be in a curriculum, what should be taught, how and when is not an easy task.

When we think of the word curriculum we often think about the National Curriculum. The National Curriculum (for Key Stage 1 and 2, 2013) and Early Years Foundation Stage Framework (2025) do not, however, act as a curriculum in the sense of telling us specifically what to teach and when to teach it. These documents act as a high-level framework and set out a structure which guides curriculum design but do not specify full content. They leave room for professional interpretation as to specific content and progression of knowledge and skills, which teachers need to provide for in long and medium-term plans.

In England, the National Curriculum governing Key Stage 1 and 2 was last revised in 2013. At the time of writing, it has just been reviewed in the recent Curriculum and Assessment Review (2025). The review recommended changes to the programme of study in Key Stage 1 and 2 in art and design to 'clarify and exemplify the knowledge and skills pupils should develop' (Curriculum and Assessment Review, 2025, 57). This is in direct response to the concern that the lack of detail in the National Curriculum can be a barrier for non-specialist primary teachers. Changes to the National Curriculum are due to be implemented in September 2028.

While the current English National Curriculum is very general, it does provide guidance about how art and design at Key Stage 1 and 2 should be a blend of:

- Acquiring knowledge and skills to be able to *create* art using creative, imaginative and reflective capabilities.
- Developing the ability to think critically and *learn about* art from a variety of cultures.

In summary, it specifies that pupils should learn about key concepts in art, different types and creators of art, a range of processes (analysis, exploration, observation and evaluation) and a variety of skills using a range of materials.

Ofsted's research review (2023) elaborates on what a high-quality curriculum includes and may guide the more detailed knowledge and skills specification suggested by the Curriculum Review (DfE, 2025).

The statutory framework for the Early Years Foundation Stage (DfE, 2025), also reflects how the subject is a blend of creating art and learning about art through engaging with art made by others. It outlines 'expressive arts and design' as a specific area of learning. It stipulates that pupils should engage with and explore a range of materials and media, safely using a variety of different tools and techniques. As with the National Curriculum for Key Stage 1 and 2, it pinpoints the importance of the processes of exploration, experimentation and evaluation.

Art and design as a discipline

The National Curriculum refers to art, design *and* craft. The Ofsted research review states 'it is not easy to draw a clear line' between these areas, 'because the boundaries between them have changed over time; these fields continue to inform and enrich each other' (2023).

Including design and craft in the definition of the subject implies a definition of the visual arts that encompasses areas which might traditionally have been excluded from a definition of 'high art'. By referring to these three areas the National Curriculum is inclusive of a wide variety of media and practices. NSEAD's magazine 'AD' of Spring 2026 devoted a whole issue to the position of design in the subject, which observes these three areas are all 'deeply involved with visual image creation, but in very different ways and for different purposes' (Gast, 2026, 16). Inclusion of such a variety is indicative of how the discipline has shifted and evolved, and continues to do so. What is the consequence of this definition when planning a curriculum? It suggests that we should ensure there are a broad range of materials and practices which pupils can experience and gather expertise in. The National Curriculum only specifically refers to drawing, painting and sculpture but refers to 'other art, craft and design techniques', implying that schools should explore other areas rather than only the three techniques expressly identified. NSEAD (2019) lists other media/practices which can be included:

- printmaking
- ceramics
- textiles
- collage

- creative craft
- photography and lens-based media
- installation
- design and graphic design
- digital and new media.

Knowledge in art

We have seen that the National Curriculum (2013) provides a framework, rather than detailed specification of what we should teach. The question, then, remains: how do we determine what we should teach?

You may have heard of the idea that a curriculum should include 'powerful knowledge'. This expression refers to subject-specific, systematic knowledge that goes beyond a person's everyday experience (Young et al., 2014). 'Systematic' in this context means that knowledge can be the basis for ideas with general application, going beyond a specific context. An example in art might be teaching about the concept of 'style' which can be applied across the curriculum. The idea of powerful knowledge is associated with social mobility: regardless of the background or social standing, pupils have an educational right to powerful knowledge. It has become a 'curriculum principle' for schools (Burns, 2018).

Let's consider what 'powerful knowledge' means in art and design. A concept of 'knowledge' in art sometimes causes anxiety. This stems from the idea that 'knowledge' and 'creativity' are opposing forces. This represents a narrow view of knowledge in art, where 'knowledge' only relates to facts rather than the practice of processes or skills. A broader view of knowledge in art combines all of these elements.

Ofsted's research review series (2023) categorises 'knowledge' in art into three domains:

- **Practical knowledge** – 'about developing technical proficiency'.
- **Theoretical knowledge** – 'the cultural and contextual content that pupils learn about artists and artwork'.
- **Disciplinary knowledge** – 'what pupils learn about how art is studied, discussed and judged'.

Let's explore these in turn.

Practical knowledge

Practical knowledge is learning methods, techniques and processes to be able to create art.

You may be thinking that the term 'practical knowledge' seems very much like what we might call 'skills' – and I would agree. The words 'knowledge' and 'skills' are sometimes seen in education as opposing ideas, where knowledge is perceived as somehow superior to skills. This stems from a departure from what educationalists refer to a 'skills-based curricula' towards 'knowledge-rich curricula'. Objection to a 'skills-based curricula', however, very much stems from practice of teaching generic skills, where subject-specific knowledge is de-emphasised (Newmark, n.d.).

In his discussion about education and 'transferable skills' such as communication, creativity, critical thinking and problem solving, Dylan Wiliam highlights the importance of subject-specific knowledge. He connects subject-specific knowledge to creativity: 'someone once described creativity as making novel selections from well-stocked shelves, and that is why creativity requires having a lot of knowledge about the field in which one wants to be creative' (Wiliam, 2025).

One of the defining features of art and design, as a school subject, is that it is practical. It is about creation. Part of subject-specific 'powerful knowledge' in art is that pupils learn the methods, techniques and processes for making art. This is integral to the subject.

Methods and techniques

Methods and techniques in art are generally particular to different areas of making: 'each has its own materials, media and technical language as part of a specialist tradition' (Ofsted, 2023). Making progress in art is in part about learning how to use materials with increasing facility across the different areas of making, set out on page 25 in 'Art and design as a discipline'. This is sometimes referred to as 'material literacy' (Briggs, 2025). Chapter 9 looks at some of the key media and basic principles relating to drawing, painting and sculpting, which pupils may use at primary school.

The elements of art

By practising and developing skills with a range of media, pupils develop what has been called 'productive expertise' (Ofsted, 2023). Part of practical knowledge, however, also relates to what has been called 'receptive expertise'.

This includes learning about concepts/ideas which are the building blocks of art, often called the 'elements' of art. These are explicitly referred to in the English National Curriculum (DfE, 2013). They are:

- line
- colour
- tone (how light or dark something is; you might see this referred to as 'value')
- shape (two-dimensional shape which has height and width)
- form (three-dimensional form which has height, wide and depth; artists can create the illusion of a three-dimensional form in two-dimensions)
- space (space between and around objects; artists can create the illusion of space in two-dimensions using techniques such as perspective; space in two-dimensional art is often referred to as foreground, middle ground and background)
- texture (using actual texture; using materials to imply texture called 'visual texture')
- pattern.

These elements relate to, and inform the creation of art. For example, by drawing, pupils will learn about and use a variety of drawing materials to create lines, patterns, shapes, different tones, illusions of light, space and texture. By painting, pupils will explore colour theory by colour mixing and create the illusion of form, space and texture through the marks they make with a brush or other painting tool. By sculpting pupils can learn about form, the importance of scale, space, colour, texture and pattern by creating objects with a variety of materials.

Design (or composition) in art means how the different elements of art work together to make a piece of art. Understanding this concept can also inform a pupil's creation of art. For example, when children study and understand how colour and shape interact they can use this knowledge in their own work. Making abstract collages with colourful paper to experiment with compositions using organic shapes and complementary colours could be one way of doing this.

Processes to create art

Practical knowledge in art and design does not only include the development of skills using a variety of media. It also includes developing knowledge of the processes undertaken to create art. These have been called 'process skills'

(Gregory et al., 2020). They are described using a variety of words in the National Curriculum for England (DfE, 2013) but can be distilled to:

- looking
- analysing
- exploring/experimenting
- inventing
- designing/planning
- evaluating.

'Process skills' are not explicitly referred to in Ofsted's research review (2023), however, reference is made to some of them at different points in the document. My view is that they form an important part of the knowledge that pupils develop as they study and make art. It is helpful to explicitly categorise them to ensure that they are included in any curriculum. They are discussed in depth in Chapters 6 and 8.

Theoretical knowledge

A rich network of knowledge can be developed if practical knowledge is connected with theoretical knowledge. Theoretical knowledge means knowledge of artists, craftworkers, designers, their work, the tools and materials with which they make art, its cultural context and concepts that relate to their work.

Bridget Green emphasises the importance of combining theoretical knowledge with practical knowledge to create an inclusive curriculum. She expresses concern at the lack of theoretical knowledge taught in schools (Green, 2021).

Theoretical knowledge is not just about knowing names and dates. The English National Curriculum states pupils should 'know about great artists, craft makers and designers, and understand the historical and cultural development of their art forms' (DfE, 2013).

Theoretical knowledge allows pupils to access and understand art from a wide range of styles, ideas and movements. A key part of developing this understanding is for pupils to look at and analyse what they see. This is discussed in detail in Chapter 6. Analysis allows pupils to look critically at art, and 'make connections between [its] past, present and future' (Ofsted, 2023). Developing a historical and cultural understanding, which explores connections, influences, themes and meanings, allows pupils to make sense of art throughout time and across the globe.

Pupils can use the elements of art to analyse what they see as well as using these concepts to guide their own practice. For example, the artist Edvard Munch is commonly regarded as an exponent of expressionism, a movement in which artists sought to express emotions rather than physical reality. By analysing his famous work *The Scream* (1893, National Museum, Oslo), pupils explore how Munch's use of swirling lines and complementary colours creates an image that conveys an unsettled feeling.

Disciplinary knowledge

Disciplinary knowledge in art has been described as 'how art is studied, discussed and judged' (Ofsted, 2023). Part of this is understanding that the discipline and study of art involves different roles and institutions: artists, designers, artisans, critics, scholars, curators, museums, galleries and community spaces. It also means understanding that definitions of art have varied over time, and that it can be created, valued and judged in different ways. This has been described as the 'plurality of art, craft, design and associated traditions' (Ofsted, 2023) – it is a fluid and dynamic discipline.

Part of disciplinary knowledge in art and design is understanding *what* artists/craftworkers/designers (who I refer to below as 'artists') do and what they create, *why* they do it and *how* they do it.

For example, take *what* artists do and what they create:

- Art exists in a huge variety of media and practices: far from being limited to drawing and painting (which are probably the categories that pupils will think about first) it can include sculpture, prints, textiles, photography, collage, ceramics, furniture, other 'functional' objects, architecture, video, installation and digital art.
- We might also consider the subject matter which artists seek to portray. This might include seeking to portray the natural world; people; buildings; stories; historical events; characters; decorative patterns; abstract images; or actions/ideas/concepts like 'movement', 'strength' or 'play'.
- We might also consider the style which artists use and whether this is particular to a time, culture, movement or idea. How do artists use the materials which they have chosen to use? How do they combine the elements of art to create a coherent design?

If we consider the purpose of art, or *why* artists do what they do, we might encounter art which:

- seeks to depict precisely what we see
- seeks to show an idealised world
- has a religious purpose
- has a political or ideological purpose
- seeks to convey emotion
- seeks to convey beauty
- is for purely decorative purposes.

If we consider *how* artists do what they do, we might encounter artists who:

- produce work by observing what they see
- work from their imagination
- produce sketches from which they plan and produce a final piece
- work 'intuitively', working on a piece directly 'in the moment' without planning.

Case study: Implementing disciplinary knowledge in the curriculum

Mrs Young, an art lead in a school in South Yorkshire, has been researching disciplinary knowledge in art. She wants to ensure that pupils are learning disciplinary knowledge throughout the curriculum.

As a start, she audits the existing planning for Year 5 and Year 6 to see where there are opportunities for highlighting disciplinary knowledge within the existing curriculum. She finds some of examples which illustrate some of the different purposes of art. These include:

Chinese painting and ceramics	Printmaking
• Traditional Chinese brush painting, used on paper and ceramics, often sought to present an idealised version of nature.	• Printmaking allows the creation of multiple versions of the same design and has therefore often been used to produce cheap and socially influential works of art which can be bought by many people.
Photography	**Impressionism and post-Impressionism**
• Photography can be used for different purposes. Documentary photography can record and represent a 'real' scene. In contrast, photography can be presented as 'art'.	• The Impressionists are known for painting landscapes and scenes from everyday life, which they often painted outside. They often sought to express the transient effects of weather and light. • The post-Impressionists are known for expressing emotion, painting from the imagination and prioritising form and the painted surface over reality.

On reflection Mrs Young decides that the curriculum should include more emphasis on craft/design and its varying purposes. In her long-term plan she maps out the disciplinary knowledge that could feature in two new units: 'Style in art' and 'Islamic art and architecture', detailed below. She will add practical and theoretical knowledge to these two units before discussing how they can be implemented with Year 5 and Year 6 staff.

Style in art: a comparison of rococo and modernism	Islamic art and architecture
• Rococo style in art is known for being pretty and light-hearted, whereas the modernist style rejected the use of decoration and ornament, favouring simplicity. This can be seen in chair design. • Rococo furniture used elaborate decoration, often based on curved natural forms which were asymmetrical. Modernist furniture design rejected the use of decoration and ornament, favouring simplicity.	• Islamic art can refer to art contained in religious books, manuscripts or buildings. It can also refer to art which is contained in secular books, manuscripts or buildings which come from an Islamic culture. • Features of Islamic art and design include geometric patterns, vegetal patterns and calligraphy (which are often words/phrases from the Koran). If used in a religious building, Islamic art is not permitted to contain images of people or animals.

Making connections

We have explored the different domains of knowledge in art. These domains are not learned in isolation. Pupils learn by making connections between them.

As we have seen in Chapter 2, schemas act as mental frameworks that store and categorise knowledge in the long-term memory. They make it easier for us to assimilate and process new, related information. The more interconnected our existing knowledge structures are, the more efficiently we can make sense of and organise new information. This not only aids comprehension of new concepts but fosters an understanding of the relationships between different pieces of information.

What does this mean in practice? We learn more easily when we make connections between schemas. A curriculum, therefore, should not present different areas of knowledge in isolation. Pupils develop 'knowledge networks' (Neuman et al, 2014) which, in art, allow them to make connections between encountering other peoples' art and what they themselves create. Children make progress in art:

- by connecting what they see in other people's work
- through concepts and ideas about art (such as analysing style by reference to the elements of art)
- by understanding how artists work and use different materials
- by understanding that artists make art for different purposes and to portray different things
- through the development of skills, techniques and processes in their own work.

Making these connections increases their own knowledge which, in turn, fosters their own creativity.

In practice: making connections between different areas of knowledge

Let's explore how an individual lesson might incorporate practical, theoretical and disciplinary knowledge. In Year 2, pupils have been learning about Matisse's collages, known as 'cut-outs'. They have already learned that: Matisse made colourful pictures by cutting out and arranging shapes; Matisse said making the pictures was like 'painting with scissors'; he made the cut-outs when he was old and ill.

In this lesson, the pupils look at the collage *Panel with Mask* (1947, Designmuseum, Denmark). They then cut out organic shapes which they stick on a background to create their own collage. The following table outlines the theoretical, disciplinary and practical knowledge in the lesson.

Theoretical knowledge	Disciplinary knowledge	Practical knowledge
• One of Matisse's cut-outs is called *Panel with Mask* which was made in 1947. • Matisse used organic shapes and complementary colours in his cut-outs. We can see this in *Panel with Mask*. • Organic shapes often appear in nature. These are shapes we cannot name – they are the opposite of geometric shapes. • Complementary colours are pairs of colours that are opposite each other on the colour wheel. They appear very bright when placed next to each other. They are always a primary colour (e.g. blue) paired with a secondary colour (e.g. orange).	• Artists can use a variety of processes to create their work. • Matisse made his 'cut-outs' sitting in his wheelchair when he was ill. He had stopped painting because this was too difficult due to the state of his health. • He cut out organic shapes from brightly coloured paper. He then directed his assistant to pin the shapes onto the wall which allowed him to carefully consider and alter the compositions he created.	• Select paper, some in complementary colours. • Draw organic shapes of different sizes on the paper. • Cut out the shapes, holding scissors with thumb and forefinger and cutting along the edge of the shape with long strokes of the scissors. • Place shapes on a background colour before sticking them down. Carefully consider the composition: how will you place differently sized shapes? What colours will be next to each other? How much space will there be around the shapes?

Making curriculum choices: depth and breadth

Writing a curriculum is all about making choices. How do we, when putting together a curriculum, choose from the vast number of artists, styles, types of art, ways of working, techniques, skills and processes which make up the constantly evolving discipline? Especially when we have limited time and resources in the primary classroom.

The Ofsted research review recognises the difficulty: 'The possible content is vast and subject leaders and curriculum designers need to be selective in what they include in their art curriculums.' (2023) How do we make these important choices? You may have heard the phrase that we should teach 'the best that has been thought and said' (Arnold, 1869). Who decides what is best, how they decide it, and by what criteria can, of course, involve difficulty.

Christine Counsell sees pupils' understanding of the characteristics of a discipline, or disciplinary knowledge, as the key. When pupils learn disciplinary knowledge they learn how a discipline is established and how it can continue to be revised. This implies that 'what I teach is not all there is' (Counsell, 2018a). We have seen how art is a continually developing and shifting domain, driven by changes in culture, ideologies and technologies. If pupils have a clear idea that *what* artists do, *why* they do it and *how* they do it has shifted over time and varies across the world, then they will in turn appreciate the variability of the domain. They will understand that what they learn is not the whole, but a selection of the whole.

If pupils are to appreciate the varied and rich nature of art, a curriculum needs to have breadth. You may have heard the expression that a curriculum should be 'a mirror' and 'a window': in other words, to connect with what they learn children should see themselves in it, as well as have their knowledge expanded beyond their own experience and culture. This is a difficult tightrope to walk, but there is no doubt that a curriculum should have breadth. It should not just be a reflection of our own, favourite choices: 'a private playlist' (Didau, 2025). Instead, it should be a carefully considered balanced representation: 'a public inheritance' (Didau, 2025).

What then, is breadth in art? It can encompass breadth in the media that pupils use. It can include breadth in how pupils use those materials, whether learning established techniques or experimenting and exploring how those materials can be used for their own expressive ends. It can mean: looking at and learning about artists and art that comes from different times and cultures; art made from different materials; art made in different ways; art made for different purposes and art made to show a variety of things. Chapter 4 explores how this breadth can be successfully and coherently incorporated into a curriculum.

In addition to breadth, an art curriculum needs opportunities for depth of study. Without depth, a broad curriculum can be like a superficial tour, where engagement is surface level. Opportunities for depth can be created by focusing study on one artist, one artwork or ways of working with one medium.

Giving pupils sufficient time to look at and discuss individual works (see Chapter 6) allows them to thoroughly engage with pieces of art and develop a deeper understanding which connects theory, discipline and practice.

It is also important that depth of study is developed by pupils concentrating on certain techniques and skills, so that they become proficient in them. The Ofsted research review recognises that 'a school art curriculum is unlikely to be able to cover all the areas of making in sufficient depth for pupils to engage meaningfully with them' (2023). Pupils will need repeated practice using certain materials so that they develop 'material literacy' (Briggs, 2025). This should include learning established techniques as well as being given the opportunity to explore and experiment (see Chapter 8). Core skills in drawing, painting and sculpture, which can be explored throughout the course of a curriculum, are discussed in Chapter 9.

Specification and sequencing

Whatever curriculum choices we make, it is fundamental that the content is adequately specified and sequenced so that pupils build knowledge and skills as they progress through it.

A curriculum needs to set out what we want pupils to learn, and when they should learn it. Michael Fordham refers to it as a journey that '…*models* the progress that we would hope (although cannot guarantee) that someone will make. The curriculum *is* the progression model' (Fordham, 2020).

Specifying what is to be learned, and in what order, is important because of what we know about how we learn from cognitive science. Bartlett's schema theory shows us how we connect new learning with existing knowledge: we need background knowledge to connect with and understand new knowledge (Bartlett, 1932). Part of doing this successfully is starting by remembering what we already know (retrieval), thereby activating prior knowledge. Sweller's cognitive load theory tells us that when we do this it reduces the cognitive load on our working memory and frees us up to make connections with new material (Sweller, 2012).

As we have seen, a good art curriculum should allow pupils to learn practical, theoretical and disciplinary knowledge and make connections between these three areas. This means knowing, understanding *and* learning how to do things, building on knowledge and skills year on year. This requires specifying and planning in each lesson, unit and for each year what practical, theoretical and disciplinary knowledge a pupil will learn, making sure that connects with what they have previously learned. Drafting a curriculum requires a whole school approach, where what is learned in Key Stage 2 connects to and develops what has been learned in Key Stage 1 and the Early Years before that. We will discuss how to do this in practice in Chapter 4.

Ambition and inclusivity

We have seen that 'powerful knowledge' goes beyond a person's everyday experience. It has been described as a 'curriculum principle' for schools in disadvantaged contexts: whatever someone's background they should be provided with the opportunity to engage with an education which provides them with 'powerful knowledge' (Burns, 2018). This is why, as subject leads, whatever our school context, ensuring that we have a knowledge-rich, specified, sequenced art and design curriculum which is taught to all children is important. We are the gateway for opportunity in our schools.

This opportunity should be inclusive of pupils who have special educational needs or any barriers to learning. This means that we should not alter or adjust the curriculum content which pupils encounter. The Ofsted research review emphasises this approach: 'Research shows that pupils with SEND do not generally benefit from differentiated teaching, activities or resources to achieve a curriculum goal' (Ofsted, 2023). This is also reinforced by the new Ofsted framework which guides schools to have a curriculum that is 'ambitious, broad and balanced, informed by the best available evidence, and designed to give all learners…the knowledge they need to achieve and thrive in later life' (Ofsted, 2025, 17).

A curriculum should allow all learners to access it with minimal need for adaptations. Unfortunately, basic access to the curriculum for pupils with additional needs can suffer: art and design, seen by some as a peripheral subject, can be side-lined so that pupils with additional needs can be taken out of art lessons to do interventions in English or maths. This restricts the opportunity for those children to engage meaningfully with the subject. As subject leads we need to work with those in senior leadership to ensure that this doesn't happen. Ensuring that art is on the timetable at the same time each week and communicating with *all* staff that the expectation is that *all* pupils take part is one way of mitigating the risk. Discussing the importance of art in a staff meeting about the importance of art in the curriculum can also be successful. A useful resource here is Thomson and Malloy's report (NSEAD, 2022) which summarises areas of benefit.

Opportunity for pupils with additional needs to fully engage with the curriculum may also be affected by the expectations that teachers have of them. The first teacher standard is that teachers should 'set high expectations which inspire, motivate and challenge' (DfE, 2011, 10). We need to ensure, in our schools, that teachers' expectations of children are always high. This is particularly pertinent in the subject of art. If a child struggles with reading, writing or numeracy this does not mean that they will also find a subject like art challenging. In fact, my experience is that children often surprise us: those who struggle in other areas of the curriculum may excel in art.

Example PD session: discussing breadth and depth of knowledge in a curriculum

Here is an example of a PD session where teachers discuss how to add value and cover a wide breadth of knowledge by sharing ideas across year groups.

TIMING SUGGESTION	SESSION GUIDANCE

5 mins	• Remind teachers that effective curriculum design is about planning carefully sequenced learning that allows pupils to revisit and deepen core knowledge over time.
	• Emphasise that good sequencing supports:
	  • progression of practical skills (e.g. mark making → drawing with control → observational drawing → imaginative composition)
	  • progression of knowledge (e.g. using vocabulary → understanding elements of art → applying these intentionally)
	  • progression of creative thinking (e.g. experimenting → refining ideas → evaluating and adapting work).
	• Explain that this mirrors the principles outlined in curriculum research:
	  • Building learning in small, connected steps.
	  • Returning to key concepts (colour, line, shape, tone, form, texture, pattern) in increasingly sophisticated ways.
	  • Ensuring that pupils learn both breadth (a wide range of experiences) and depth (mastery over time).

10 mins	Explain the key principles to consider when designing and sequencing a primary art curriculum.
	
	1. Revisiting core concepts with greater depth each time:
	  • Pupils re-encounter the same art concepts (colour, line, shape, tone, form, texture, pattern) with greater complexity each year.
	2. Skills progression:
	  • Art skills (e.g., drawing, painting, printing, sculpture, textiles, digital art) build step-by-step so that pupils can see clear development.
	3. Sequencing knowledge of artists:
	  • Exposure to diverse artists progresses from simple recognition to contextual understanding to analysis to influencing pupil's own work.

	4. Techniques and media have a rationale for order: • Materials are introduced in a structured way so pupils practise foundational techniques before applying them independently. 5. Vocabulary and critical language grows over time: • Pupils learn to describe, analyse and evaluate art using increasingly sophisticated vocabulary. Using a visualiser or slides, show an example of a single concept, e.g. colour, and demonstrate how it can be sequenced across the school: • EYFS – exploring colour mixing with primary paints. • KS1 – identifying warm/cool colours, mixing tints and shades and secondary colours and using them intentionally. • Lower KS2 – using different tones/hues to show form. • Upper KS2 – using colour to convey emotion or symbolism in their own compositions.

15 mins	• Working in pairs or small groups, combine teachers from different year groups or key stages with each other so they can discuss sequencing skills across year groups.
	• Ask teachers to bring a unit they are currently teaching or will teach soon.
	• Teachers should discuss:
	  • What prior knowledge and skills pupils need before this unit.
	  • What this unit adds to pupils' knowledge and skills.
	  • How this learning will be built on in the next year group.
	• Ask pairs to map a simple progression line on paper for one of the following:
	  • drawing
	  • painting
	  • printing
	  • sculpture.

5 mins	• Ask each pair to share one insight with the group.
	• They might identify:
	  • **Two elements of strong sequencing** in the current curriculum.
	  • **One area that needs refining** (e.g. a skill introduced too early/late, or gaps between year groups).

Chapter summary

- Art and design is a continually evolving discipline that includes a broad range of media and practices.
- A curriculum is what we intend to teach. It should provide, with specificity, what we teach and when we teach it.

- The National Curriculum is a high-level framework which specifies that pupils should acquire knowledge and skills to be able to *create* art and develop the ability to think critically and *learn about* art from a variety of cultures.
- Knowledge in art can be categorised as practical, theoretical and disciplinary. Pupils learn by making connections between these three areas of knowledge.
- An effective art curriculum will have both depth and breadth of knowledge.
- An effectively designed art curriculum should allow all pupil access to it, with minimal need for adaptations.

Questions for reflection

- Does the curriculum that we presently follow specify the practical, theoretical, disciplinary knowledge that pupils learn in a unit of work?
- Is it broadly designed to build practical, theoretical and disciplinary knowledge, year on year?
- How does it meet the requirements of having breadth and depth?
- Do all pupils, whatever their background and educational needs, have access to the same curriculum?

Explore further

- NSEAD's explanation the National Curriculum, which defines key vocabulary: www.nsead.org/static/index.html
- NSEAD's response to Ofsted's research review series for art and design: www.nsead.org/files/9f1311767d7a5252766fe2a266f1e78e.pdf
- Chrisine Counsell's article 'Taking curriculum seriously': www.my.chartered.college/impact_article/taking-curriculum-seriously
- Ben Newmark's blog 'The best that has been thought and said?': www.bennewmark.wordpress.com/2019/05/24/the-best-that-has-been-thought-and-said

4 Designing a curriculum

This chapter explores how we can put the principles discussed in Chapter 3 into practice. Designing a curriculum involves making deliberate choices about content, progression and structure so that pupils revisit content and deepen core ideas over time. We will examine what an ambitious, inclusive, specified and well-sequenced art and design curriculum looks like. We will also discuss how to incorporate practical, theoretical and disciplinary knowledge. This will help you to ensure that your school's art curriculum dedicates appropriate time and space to hands-on making, understanding artistic concepts and techniques and developing pupils' awareness of the wider traditions, contexts and purposes of art and design.

We will consider:

- practicalities of drafting a curriculum
- curriculum structure
- curriculum choices – diversity
- specificity of content and progression across year groups.

Practicalities

Making decisions about what should be taught and when it should be taught (whether by considering the suitability of a whole scheme, using a variety of sources or by developing a curriculum from scratch), should not be the sole responsibility of the subject lead. These decisions should be taken cooperatively between middle and senior leaders. The process should also be influenced by teachers who deliver the curriculum through a continual cycle of assessment and monitoring (discussed further in Chapter 10).

What does this mean in practice? A subject lead, perhaps making use of a variety of outside sources (such as those detailed in the 'Explore further' section at the end of this chapter), might produce an outline structure which sets out how practical, theoretical and disciplinary knowledge progresses from the Early Years to Year 6. Such a document can specify what different methods, techniques, processes, concepts, art and artists pupils encounter during the course of a year. This overview can become the backbone of the content.

It is then presented in individual lessons over the course of a half-term unit and developed collaboratively between subject leads and teachers.

Working in this way ensures that a subject lead maps out a coherent vision, and a curriculum that builds from year to year, whilst the input of senior leaders and teachers provides a moderating influence as to suitability and range of content.

Case study: Year 2 curriculum overview

This example overview plan for Year 2, from the Primary Knowledge Curriculum, details what artists, concepts, skills and processes are incorporated into six units over the course of a year (Primary Knowledge Curriculum, 2025). The concepts listed cover aspects of both theoretical and disciplinary knowledge. It acts as an outline for more detailed planning produced for each unit.

Autumn A	Autumn B	Spring A	Spring B	Summer A	Summer B
Colour and shape *Artists*: Monet, Klee, Kandinsky, Delaunay, Picasso, Kelly, Calder. *Concepts*: primary colours, secondary colours, warm and cool colours, tints and shades, geometric shapes, organic shapes, different applications of paint and shape can create different moods and effects. *Skills:* colour mixing, drawing geometric shapes, using natural objects to draw organic shapes, creating sculptures with paper and wire, working as a team. *Processes*: analysing/looking, experimentation and invention, design and planning, working by observation.	**Colour, shape and texture** *Artists*: Jan van Eyck, Durer, Matisse, Mukherjee. *Concepts*: collaged cut-outs, organic shapes, composition, visual texture, how artists can work in different ways. *Skills*: colour mixing, selecting colours, cutting organic shapes, creating texture with mark making and colour, drawing with chalk and charcoal, graphite and oil pastels. *Processes*: analysing/looking, experimentation and invention, design and planning, working by observation.	**Portraits and self-portraits** *Artists*: Leonardo da Vinci, Holbein, Gentileschi, Hogarth, Rembrandt, Van Gogh, Kahlo, Picasso, Kehinde Wiley, Lynnette Yiadom-Boadkye. *Concepts*: portraits/ self-portraits, representation in portraits, simple proportions of a face, cubism, working from the imagination. *Skills*: planning and drawing a face, drawing a profile, mixing skin tones, drawing with oil pastels. *Processes*: analysing/ looking, experimentation and invention, design and planning, working by observation.	**Landscape and symmetry** *Artists*: Landscape – Constable, Turner, Rousseau, Uzo Egonu. *Symmetry* – Leonardo da Vinci, Hobbema, Goldsworthy, Adam Hillman. *Concepts*: What is a landscape? What is a seascape? Urban landscapes, using different methods to paint landscapes. Symmetry in nature and art, natural and manmade materials, temporary art. *Skills*: washes with a sponge, using bold brushstrokes, detailed drawing with oil pastels, creating sculptures with found objects. *Processes*: analysing/looking, experimentation and invention, design and planning, working by observation.	**Narrative art** *Artists*: Antonio del Pollaiuolo, Pelagi, Kauffman, Burne-Jones, Picasso. *Concepts*: mythological paintings, narrative art, settings, showing different characteristics of a character. *Skills*: sketching, using a ruler, drawing different characteristics, using chalk and charcoal to create tone, collage. *Processes*: analysing/ looking, experimentation and invention, design and planning, working by observation.	**Murals and tapestries** *Artists/Art*: Michelangelo, Leonardo da Vinci, Rego, *The Lady and the Unicorn* tapestries, Banksy. *Concepts*: what is a mural? What is a tapestry? Using art to communicate stories and messages, composition. *Skills*: mono-printing, weaving, creating a composition on a wall. *Processes*: analysing/ looking,design and planning, working by observation, working in a group.

Curriculum structure

As we have explored, we learn more easily when we make connections between schemas. An art and design curriculum, therefore, should not present different areas of knowledge in isolation but take an integrated approach. Pupils make progress in art by:

- connecting what they see in other people's work
- connecting concepts and ideas about art (such as analysing style by reference to the elements of art)
- understanding how artists work and use different materials
- understanding that artists make art for different purposes and to portray different things
- developing skills, techniques and processes in their own work.

Individual lessons and groups of lessons (units) in art and design may combine some or all of these factors. Different units may have one particular area as their focus but integrate other areas of knowledge throughout a series of lessons.

Individual units might focus on:

- different concepts/ideas, e.g. the elements of art such as 'colour' or 'line' or the idea of 'style'
- different media, e.g. individual units on drawing, painting, sculpture, printmaking, textiles, photography, ceramics or collage
- different types of subject, e.g. narrative art, portraiture, landscapes, still life or abstract art
- art from different times and cultures, e.g. Anglo-Saxon art, Victorian architecture, modernism, Chinese painting and ceramics, Islamic art
- different movements in art, e.g. Impressionism, expressionism or the arts and crafts movement
- a particular artist.

In practice: suggested focus for different units of work

Let's consider how these different focusses might appear at each different key stage. The table below details focuses for different units of work, to give you an idea of the range of possibilities with different ages groups.

Early Years	Key Stage 1

• Concepts such as:
  • colour (naming colours, bright/dull colours, identifying the primary colours, mixing secondary colours)
  • line and pattern (naming lines, creating repeated patterns).
• Using different materials such as:
  • drawing materials (pencil, charcoal, chalk, oil pastels)
  • painting materials (ready mixed paints, watercolours, brushes, sponges, finger-painting)
  • sculpture/collage materials (natural objects, air-dry clay, junk modelling and creating different textures with these materials)
  • simple printing techniques using found/natural objects, hands/feet.
• Different subject matter/art for different purposes such as:
  • nature
  • people
  • art which tells stories.
	• Concepts such as:
	  • colour (warm/cool, tints/shades)
	  • line (lines can make shapes)
	  • shape (geometric/organic)
	  • texture (creating an illusion of texture by drawing)
	  • symmetry in art
	  • contrasting styles in art (e.g. in relation to particular media such as painting or sculpture).
	• Art defined by different media such as:
	  • murals
	  • sculpture
	  • printmaking (creating relief prints from materials like polystyrene).
	• Different subject matter/art for different purposes such as:
	  • portraits (proportions of the face, representation in portraits)
	  • landscapes
	  • narrative art.

Lower Key Stage 2	**Upper Key Stage 2**

• Concepts such as:
  • line (different ways of using line)
  • colour (complementary and analogous colours, using colour to show emotion/expression)
  • form (how we can create the illusion of three-dimensional form in two dimensions)
  • light (using light to show form, using light to create drama)
  • space (using colour and detail to create the illusion of space in a picture – foreground, middle ground and background)
  • design (how artists combine the different elements of art to create a design).
	• Concepts such as:
	  • style (comparing two contrasting styles)
	  • realism/naturalism
	  • abstraction.
	• Art defined by different media such as:
	  • printmaking (relief printing, screen printing)
	  • photography
	  • installation art
	  • digital art.

• Different subject matter/art for different purposes such as:
  • still life (proportions of the face, representation in portraits)
  • art to portray an emotional response (e.g. expressionism).
• Art defined by different media such as:
  • ceramics
  • textiles (e.g. embroidery/weaving)
• Art from different times/cultures such:
  • Anglo-Saxon manuscripts and decorative works in metal
  • Byzantine mosaics, decoration and icons
  • traditional and modern architecture.
• Focus on a particular artist.
	• Art from different times/cultures such as:
	  • Renaissance art/architecture
	  • Islamic art and architecture
	  • traditional Chinese painting and ceramics
	  • art from Western Africa (e.g. Benin Bronzes, art from Mali)
	  • modernism.
	• Different movements in art such as:
	• Impressionism
	  • post-impressionism
	  • the Pre-Raphaelites
	  • expressionism
	  • abstract expressionism
	  • neo-expressionism
	  • Cubism
	  • pop art
	  • minimalism
	  • conceptual art
	  • street art
	  • green art.
	• Focus on a particular artist.

Curriculum choices: diversity

We have seen in Chapter 3 that art is a continually developing and shifting domain, and how breadth of study is needed to understand that what is learned is not the whole domain, but a selection from it. Ensuring that there is diversity in a curriculum allows pupils to learn how knowledge in art is formed and how it has changed and continues to change and develop.

For pupils to understand the developing and shifting domain of art we need to ensure that there is a diverse range of content in a curriculum, from different times and cultures. This requires balance. There is a tendency, sometimes, for curriculum drafters to concentrate solely on what they think pupils will find engaging and identify with – what is seen as new or cutting edge. Of course, this is an important part of the story. However, an unbalanced focus, which ignores the rich history of art as a reflection of culture and an influencing force on society lacks depth.

To achieve breadth we can introduce pupils to a balance of art from different times, different places across the world (considering carefully what examples can be picked from 'contested and neglected stories of art' from outside Europe (Ofsted, 2023)) and artists from diverse communities.

A useful measure of 'different times' can be to split into broadly three periods:

- 'Traditional' – art produced before 'modern' art.
- 'Modern' – art from the last quarter of the nineteenth century/beginning of twentieth century beginning with Impressionism, post-Impressionism and Cubism.
- 'Contemporary' – art made by living artists today, from last quarter of the twentieth century to the present.

It is important that, whatever curriculum choices we make, we regularly review those choices and make considered adjustments. The need for continual review reflects how art and design is a fluid and developing discipline. We should consider new art and design which reflects our own contemporary society and also consider historical art and artists who may come to light, having been neglected in the past.

In practice: creating a diverse curriculum

Here are some ideas for areas of study to ensure balanced and diverse content across a curriculum.

- **Contrasting art from different times such as the 'traditional' and the 'modern'** for example, contrasting painting and furniture design from rococo and modernist styles:
  - Rococo painting: Watteau, light colours, curved lines, light-hearted.
  - Rococo furniture: Chippendale, elaborate decoration, often asymmetrical.
  - Modernist painting: Mondrian, Van Doesburg, abstract, experimental and focused on materials.
  - Modernist furniture design: Breuer, rejected ornament, favoured simplicity.

- **Exploring how art from different periods and cultures have used one of the elements of art** such as light:
  - Light to show drama – chiaroscuro (Caravaggio, 1571–1610) is an Italian term which means 'light-dark' and refers to a technique where an artist uses clear tonal contrasts to create very clear form or dramatic effect.

- Light to show photographic realism – Vermeer (1632–1875) specialised in domestic scenes of middle-class life. He is known for his astounding use of light.
- Light as the main subject of a work of art or used as a 'material'. Goncharova (1881–1962) tried to show rays of light in her paintings. Begum (contemporary) uses light like a material in her sculptures.

- **Exploring different styles used by artists from contrasting cultures/times using the same medium** such as printmaking:
  - Printing is an indirect art that can be made using a block, plate or screen.
  - William Hogarth (1697–1764) was well-known for printmaking, and made many editions reflecting life in London which could be sold relatively cheaply.
  - Katsushika Hokusai (1760–1849) made many relief wood cut prints including 36 views of Mount Fuji.
  - Andy Warhol (1928–1987) was famous for his screen-prints in the 'pop art' style. Screen-printing allows an artist to produce multiple prints with the same design but in different colours.

- **A detailed study of artwork from a particular period/culture** such as the Italian Renaissance:
  - Renaissance ('rebirth') describes the revival of art in Italy from about 1400 influenced by the rediscovery of classical art and culture. It reached its peak from about 1500–1530 in the work of Michelangelo, Raphael and Leonardo da Vinci.
  - The recovery of the artistic values of the classical period emphasised the extraordinary ability of the human mind (humanism) and artists strove to create paintings and sculptures of idealised human forms.
  - Artists also used different techniques to make their paintings more realistic. Linear perspective was used to create the illusion of space or depth on a flat surface.

- **A detailed study of specific styles/artworks from outside Europe** such as traditional Chinese painting:
  - The same materials are used to make both Chinese painting and calligraphy: solid ink is ground on a stone and applied to silk or paper which is rolled up in a scroll. Chinese calligraphy was thought of as an important art long before painting.

    - The art of calligraphy in China emphasises practice and control. In ancient China, students had to memorise many characters each week – it was thought that the brush was like an extension of the arm, and their execution showed something about the person who painted them.
    - Traditional Chinese painting has clear, defined features: paintings often only use black ink or a limited colour palette. Paintings are usually of nature; there is often nothing in the background, creating the illusion of lots of space. The design is often asymmetrical; paintings are often supposed to look idealised and simplified rather than real.

- **Exploring how different modern and contemporary artists from diverse backgrounds have explored a particular issue** such as migration and identity:
    - Frank Auerbach (1931–2024) was born in Berlin and came to London as a child to escape Nazism. He is known for figurative portraits and city scenes which are painted in very thick paint. Auerbach painted city scenes of London being rebuilt in the 1950s after the second world war.
    - Frank Bowling was born in Guyana in 1934 but has spent most of his life in Britain. He is known for his colourful abstract paintings, some of which he made by pouring. In the 1970s, staking a claim for the importance of abstract art, he resisted what he saw as the reductive categorisation of 'Black Art' as purely political in subject matter (Hauser and Wirth, 2025).
    - Lubaina Himid was born in Tanzania in 1954 and moved to Britain when she was a child. Many of her paintings concern the contributions of African migrants to European culture. Himid was part of a movement in the 1980s to create opportunities for black artists.

Specificity and progression

Chapter 3 discussed the importance of specifying and sequencing a curriculum so that pupils' knowledge and skills build as they progress through it. This means specifying and planning in each lesson, unit and for each year what practical, theoretical and disciplinary knowledge a pupil will learn and making sure that it connects with what they have previously learned. This requires a whole school approach: the knowledge that pupils gain in the Early Years needs to build gradually through Key Stage 1 and 2. Part of this means reviewing what pupils already know and can do, thereby activating prior knowledge, before moving on to new content.

As subject leads we need to ensure that the art and design curriculum which we use or develop gradually builds from year to year. We need to consider this in relation to the different kinds of knowledge, practical, theoretical and disciplinary, which make up the subject.

Building practical knowledge: methods and techniques

Part of building practical knowledge is developing methods and techniques that are particular to different areas of making. For pupils to master particular techniques, repeated practice, which gradually builds skills, needs to be incorporated in the curriculum. Pupils need to be given time to revisit what they have previously learned and given time to practise, guided by instruction, so that they can begin to perform skills with 'automaticity' (Ofsted, 2023). This means carrying out basic skills and techniques confidently and accurately without needing to think through each step.

Learning methods and techniques with different materials provides an important basis for creativity. The Ofsted research review (2023) emphasises the need to learn certain skills and techniques before exploring how to use these creatively. Others see this as too linear approach (NSEAD, 2023), implying that creative development and the development of skills may, in fact, occur concurrently. Whichever approach is taken it is clear that 'creative work does not mean that technical competence can be ignored or overruled in the name of "freedom"' (Addison et al, 2010, 45).

While repeated practice of methods and techniques is important to develop automaticity, some literature suggests that varying practice can also build expertise. When different techniques are practised in new contexts this can help build connections between different mental schemas so that pupils build a depth of proficiency and understanding (Brown et al, 2014). Examples in art and design might include making lighter/darker tones with a variety of paint types (e.g. making a colour lighter by adding white whilst using acrylics or adding water whilst using watercolours) or building up depth of colour by layering tones from dark to light in different materials, such as oil pastels and then acrylic paints.

Building practical knowledge: processes

Practical knowledge in art and design does not only include the development of skills using a variety of media but also includes developing knowledge of the processes undertaken to create art (looking, analysing, exploring/experimenting, inventing, design/planning and evaluating). These are discussed in detail in Chapters 6 and 8.

It is important that a curriculum provides gradual development of the practice of these processes. Let's consider how these processes might look at different stages across the primary phase.

- Analytical and evaluative responses to questions when looking at art, in the Early Years and at Key Stage 1, are likely to be oral. At Key Stage 2, children can begin to produce written annotations to record their observational and evaluative responses.
- The process of designing/planning is likely to be more limited in scope in the Early Years/Key Stage 1 and become more developed at Key Stage 2. For example:
  - In Key Stage 1, design and planning might take place by asking pupils to consider what they are going to do before they implement their plan in the same lesson. For example, Year 2 might place collaged shapes on a background piece of paper so that they can consider the overall composition before they stick the shapes down.
  - In Key Stage 2, pupils may begin to sketch and plan how they are going to develop a piece of work before implementing their plan. Such projects may be sustained over a number of weeks. For example, Year 5 might make observational sketches of insects then create a two-dimensional drawn plan which specifies materials and colour, before creating a cardboard relief sculpture.
- It is important for there to be specified opportunities within the curriculum for experimentation/exploration alongside practice of specified techniques. Some examples are given, in relation to painting, in the table on page 53.
- Experimentation/exploration may directly relate to, and draw upon, practice of specified techniques, for example:
  - In the Early Years, pupils may experiment with applying paint with different tools such as sponges, cotton buds or their hands/fingers alongside using brushes to develop colour mixing techniques.

- In Key Stage 1, pupils may experiment with the different effects/textures which they can create by using their brush in different ways to paint pictures of water, alongside specified practice to create smooth and rough brushstrokes.
- In Key Stage 2, pupils may experiment with the emotional effect they can create by using different colour combinations alongside learning about colour theory.

In practice: building painting skills

This table explores how painting methods and techniques might build throughout a curriculum. It demonstrates how skills build through repeated practice of the same aspects of a technique (e.g. colour mixing and brush control) and varied practice (e.g. the different ways of making lighter/darker tones with different varieties of paint). It also demonstrates how established practices can be used as a basis/springboard for experimentation (e.g. using a variety of brushstrokes to show texture).

Early Years	Key Stage 1
• Exploring different painting materials and tools: finger-painting, brushes, sponges, found materials, ready mix paint, watercolours, different consistencies of paint, experimental colour mixing. • Painting using primary colours without mixing. • Mixing colours. • Mixing primary colours to make secondary colours.	• Brush hold/control. • Brush size and choice. • Mixing secondary colours, warm/cool colours, tints and shades with ready mixed paint. • Painting with watercolour, not mixing colours. • Accurately painting inside a shape. • Using a variety of brushstrokes to show texture/creating smooth brushstrokes. • Using brushstrokes which vary in length. • Painting with tools other than a brush. • Applying washes with a sponge.
Lower Key Stage 2	**Upper Key Stage 2**
• Brush hold/control. • Brush size and choice. • Mixing secondary colours, warm/cool colours, tints and shades with ready mixed paint.	• Experimenting using different brush size and variety. • Experimenting with brush hold. • Colour choice and colour mixing using acrylics, layering acrylics from dark to light.

• Mixing skin-tones with ready mixed paint. • Working from dark to light using acrylic: add shadows with dark colours progressing through mid-tones to highlights with lighter colours. • Painting with watercolour, adding water to create lighter colours. • Accurately painting inside a shape. • Using a variety of brushstrokes to show texture/creating smooth brushstrokes. • Stippling with the brush to create an uneven effect. • Using brushstrokes which vary in length. • Using a brush to apply a simple wash. • Painting with tools other than a brush. • Applying paint evenly to a 3D object. • Keeping colours in a symmetrical pattern. • Using darker colours in the foreground and lighter colours in the background.	• Painting with a limited palette of colours. • Colour mixing with watercolour, adding water to make colours lighter. • Working in watercolour, applying layers from light to dark. • Working in watercolour, applying washes, experimenting with wet on wet, wet on dry and wax resist. • Painting using coloured inks, experimenting creating different densities of ink. • Experimenting using different brushstrokes to create different effects, varying width, pressure and speed. • Accurately painting inside a shape using smooth brushstrokes. • Experimenting with applying paint with a variety of tools. • Keeping colours in a symmetrical pattern.

Building theoretical knowledge

Theoretical knowledge means knowledge of artists, their work, the tools and materials with which they make art, its cultural context and concepts that relate to their work. Theoretical knowledge allows pupils to access and understand art from a wide range of styles, ideas and movements.

Developing historical and cultural understanding, which explores connections, influences, themes and meanings, necessitates careful sequencing of content. For example:

- **In the Early Years and Key Stage 1** exploring the idea that art can tell stories (such as pre-historic cave paintings) in Reception forms a basis for looking at narrative art in Year 1 (such as paintings which tell the story of 'George and the Dragon'). In Year 2, this progression continues with history paintings that tell classical myths and stories from the Bible.
- **In upper Key Stage 2** pupils learn about painting and sculpture in the Italian Renaissánce, which emphasised showing idealised forms influenced by classical art. They then learn about the Impressionists, who, in contrast, sought to show the transitory effects of the weather and real street scenes.

Creating a curriculum which gradually builds theoretical knowledge also entails careful sequencing of content relating to the elements of art. Knowledge of the concept of colour might build in this way:

EYFS	KS1	Lower KS2	Upper KS2
• naming colours • colours can be dull/ bright • primary colours • mixing secondary colours.	• mixing tints/ shades • mixing all of the primary colours to make brown • warm/cool colours.	• using colour to create form • complementary and analogous colours • using colours to show emotion.	• tertiary colours • using colour theory to create different effects • observing and replicating colour in nature • using colour to create the illusion of space: stronger colours in the foreground, more diffuse colours in the background.

Building disciplinary knowledge

Part of disciplinary knowledge in art is understanding *what* artists do and what they create, *why* they do it and *how* they do it. Part of building this knowledge can be developing an understanding of the different and varying purposes of art. This table explores how such knowledge might build from EYFS to KS2.

EYFS	KS1	Lower KS2	Upper KS2
• Art can tell us stories. • Art can show us how something looks. • Art can affect our feelings.	• Art can be used to tell stories or contain a message and tell us about different characters in a story. • Art can tell us about the past. • Two-dimensional art can show us how something feels (texture) using colour and line. • Portraits and self-portraits can show us what someone looks like but also show their feelings, character, status and interests.	• A work of art can use size, line, tone and colour to create an illusion of three-dimensions, space and depth in a painting. • Light can be used to show drama and realism in a work of art. • The design of a work of art can seek to create beauty or express emotion in a work of art (e.g. expressionism). • Embroidery/weaving can create decorative patterns or pictures and tell stories. • Art can be used to show the power of a civilisation.	• Art from the Italian Renaissance sought to present realistic representations of people and nature and sometimes presented idealised representations of people. • The Impressionists are known for painting landscapes showing transient weather effects and scenes from everyday life. • The post-Impressionists are known for expressing emotion and painting from the imagination and prioritising form and the painted surface over reality. • Cubism, developed at the beginning of the twentieth century is a way of painting or drawing where an artist shows more than one view of something in the same picture. • Some twentieth-century painters and sculptors created figurative art, whereas some created abstract art. • Some modern and contemporary artists have made art about identity, including works about race and gender. • Art can have a religious purpose. Islamic art can refer to art contained in religious books, manuscripts or buildings. • Photography can be used for different purposes, e.g. documentary photography, photography presented as art.

Cross-curricular links

Pupils learn by making connections between different domains of knowledge in art. In the same way, pupils also learn by making connections with concepts, ideas and skills which they learn in other subjects. Obvious connections can be made between art and history or art and geography. Making such connections deepens pupils' understanding and makes them more likely to remember what they have learned.

When designing a curriculum, therefore, it is preferable to consider effective sequencing between subjects. This does not mean diluting the subject-specific knowledge which is particular to each domain but devising ways to emphasise the connections which pupils can make. One way of doing this is to teach related content at the same time, or close in time, and highlighting related content using methods of questioning which elicit the retrieval of existing knowledge.

Example PD session: mapping cross-curricular opportunities

Here is an example of a PD session where teachers share knowledge across subjects to strengthen pupil knowledge and context.

TIMING SUGGESTION	**SESSION GUIDANCE**

5 mins	• Explain that the session will explore how collaborative planning across subjects can create a more coherent and enriching curriculum for pupils.
	• Remind teachers that cross-curricular links should:
	  • enhance the quality of art learning
	  • strengthen conceptual understanding in other subjects
	  • provide rich cultural and historical context
	  • offer pupils meaningful and real-world purposes for creating art
	  • help embed knowledge through interconnected experiences.

10 mins	• Explain how cross-curricular links should:
	  • support art skills, techniques and knowledge
	  • identify natural overlaps rather than forced connections, e.g. pattern relating to symmetry in maths
	  • share key terms and vocabulary
	  • coincide at logical moments throughout the year, e.g. planning landscape drawings near a geography trip.
	• Ask teachers to name some natural links between different subjects and art. Invite a subject lead from a different discipline to share insights.

15 mins	• Working in pairs or small groups, ask teachers to choose an upcoming art unit, e.g. portraits and self-portraits, printmaking, collage.
	• Identify natural cross-curricular opportunities by discussing and creating a simple grid with three prompts:
	  • core art skills/knowledge
	  • shared concepts or themes
	  • benefits to pupils' learning of combining subjects.

5 mins	• Ask teachers to reflect on how cross-curricular links enrich, rather than dilute the art and design curriculum.

Chapter summary

- As subject leads we need to ensure that the curriculum which we use or design gradually builds practical, theoretical and disciplinary knowledge from year to year.
- An art and design curriculum can be structured by creating units which focus on different concepts/ideas, media, time periods, cultures, movements, styles or types of subject.
- To achieve diversity in a curriculum we can introduce pupils to a balance of art from different times (traditional, modern and contemporary) across the world and created by artists from diverse communities.
- Careful sequencing can ensure the pupils deepen their understanding in art and design by making connections with other subjects.

Questions for reflection

- Do you have an overall curriculum plan, incorporating all year groups, which specifies how knowledge builds?
- How is the curriculum structured?
- Does the curriculum cover a diverse range of art and artists?
- How is the curriculum sequenced to make the most of connections with other subjects?

Explore further

- Oak/NSEAD curriculum for two units per year group specified by medium: www.nsead.org/resources/primary-education/primary-art/oak-national-academy
- Oak/NSEAD curriculum for EYFS, six units: www.thenational.academy/teachers/programmes/expressive-arts-and-design-foundation-early-years-foundation-stage-l/units
- Access Art primary art curriculum www.accessart.org.uk/primary-art-curriculum
- Primary Knowledge Curriculum primary art curriculum: www.primaryknowledgecurriculum.org/teacher-resources/art

5 What makes an effective lesson?

What are the ingredients of a good art and design lesson, or series of lessons? As subject leads, we need to actively consider what a good lesson might feature when we are observing teachers and guiding them in their practice. While there are elements which are common to teaching all subjects in the primary setting, there are also subject-specific considerations which are essential to understand and highlight to the staff we are working with. High-quality lessons are carefully structured and involve more than providing pupils with materials and time to create something. Art and design subject leads need to think about how new techniques are introduced, how pupils are supported in experimenting, and how the learning connects to the wider art curriculum. Effective lessons balance guidance with pupil independence, to allow pupils to make creative choices with the knowledge that they gain.

Chapters 6, 7 and 8 cover important aspects of teaching art (looking, guiding practice and the importance of process) separately. In this chapter we will consider:

- specifying what will be taught in a lesson
- structure of a lesson or unit
- retrieval practice
- explicit teaching – vocabulary, theoretical and disciplinary knowledge
- language, questioning and discussion
- time to practise and create
- teaching art and design in EYFS.

Specifying what will be taught in a lesson

In Chapter 4 we explored how it is important for a subject lead to set out, in outline, how practical, theoretical and disciplinary knowledge progresses from the Early Years to Year 6. This overview can be the backbone of the content which is then developed and presented by teachers in individual units or lessons. For an outline plan to be implemented effectively, it is important that teachers have a clear outline of what they want pupils to learn in each lesson, and how this is specified and structured over a series of lessons.

Here it is useful to think about 'core knowledge' and 'hinterland knowledge'. 'Core knowledge' is the essential knowledge that you want a pupil to learn, the 'residue that we want to secure in pupils' long-term memories' (Counsell, 2018). 'Hinterland knowledge' refers to the enriching contextual narrative of the curriculum which frames the core information and skills (Howard and Hill, 2000). In art, this could be the experience and understanding gained by looking at and talking about a work of art.

We might think of 'core knowledge' as comprising key pieces of practical, theoretical or disciplinary knowledge which a lesson or series of lessons seeks to impart. The core knowledge which that we want pupils to learn from a lesson can be distilled to a few salient points and specified in a lesson plan.

This does not mean that 'core knowledge' is more important than the 'hinterland knowledge' which supports it (Counsell, 2018). What might be described as 'hinterland knowledge' in art, for example, the experience of looking at a work of art, is one of the things that is enriching about the subject. Let's explore how we might specify 'core' and 'hinterland' knowledge in an art lesson with an example.

In practice: core and hinterland knowledge in a Year 4 lesson

The objective of this lesson is for pupils to learn how artists can use foreground, middle ground and background to create the illusion of depth in a painting. The table below illustrates what information, presented in a lesson plan, might be core and hinterland knowledge.

Core theoretical/ disciplinary knowledge	Core practical knowledge	Hinterland knowledge
Artists can use foreground, middle ground and background to create the illusion of depth in a painting. Foreground means the part of a view that is closest to us in a picture. Background means the part of the view that is furthest away from us in a picture. Middle ground is between the foreground and the background. Foreshortening means where an object is bigger in the foreground and smaller in the background.	*Observe:* Look at a scene out of a window. Carefully observe the forms you can see in the scene. Identify forms in the foreground, middle ground and background. Ask yourself: where do the objects appear bigger? *Draw shapes in the air:* Use your finger to draw the main shapes you can see in the air. *Sketch*: Using a soft pencil (e.g. 2b), quickly sketch the main forms that you can see in the foreground, middle ground and background, using light sketchy lines to show the outside of the shapes.	Look at and discuss Millet's painting *The Gleaners* (1857, Musée D'Orsay). In particular, discuss: • What the pupils can see in the foreground, middle ground and background. • Why the figures in the foreground are so much bigger than pupils in the background (foreshortening).

Structure of a lesson or unit

Let's now consider how specified knowledge can be taught well in a lesson. These are some of the key features that a good art lesson might include:

- retrieval practice
- explicit teaching of vocabulary, theoretical/disciplinary and practical knowledge
- questioning and discussion in response to a stimulus (for example, looking at a work of art, object, scene or learning about a story)
- time to practise and create
- pupil's evaluation of their own work.

Whether these all feature in a lesson, and in what order, will depend on the structure of an overall series of lessons in a unit of work. It is advisable to use retrieval practice and to introduce or revise vocabulary near the beginning of a lesson, so that pupils reengage with what they have learned in the past. Similarly, as art and design at primary school is defined by giving pupils the opportunity to make art, it is likely that every lesson will include the explicit teaching of practical knowledge and will also give pupils time to practise and create.

Whether each lesson incorporates questioning/discussion in response to a stimulus and teaching of new theoretical/disciplinary knowledge will depend on the course of a series of lessons. In EYFS, Key Stage 1, and to a certain extent, in earlier Key Stage 2, it is likely that practical work will consist of a series of short, connected, discrete projects, each of which can be completed during one lesson. In these circumstances each lesson can incorporate questioning/discussion in response to a stimulus and teaching of new theoretical/disciplinary knowledge. However, in older year groups, (sometimes in lower Key Stage 2 and particularly in upper Key Stage 2), where pupils have an increased stamina and capacity to develop ideas, it is likely that they may complete longer practical projects over a series of lessons. This will mean that in later lessons in a sequence, they focus their time and attention on generating ideas, and on planning and creating their own artwork rather than responding to and discussing a stimulus. In these circumstances, in a series of six lessons the main focus of each lesson might be:

1. To investigate and discuss a stimulus, such as an existing work of art,practising a practical skill in a particular medium which relates to that work.
2. To revisit the work of art discussed in lesson one, using it as a stimulus to generate and sketch ideas for their own piece of work.
3. To revisit and compare the works of art discussed in lesson one and two, take ideas generated in lesson two and create a plan for one of their ideas.
4. To work on their own artwork from their plan.
5. Continuing to work on their own artwork from their plan.
6. Finish and evaluate their own work, and that of their peers.

Let's look at some of the key features of a lesson in turn.

Case study: Characteristics of a good art lesson

Arts PKC

Space
Lesson 2:
Exploring space in painting: foreground, middle ground and background

PKC Primary Knowledge Curriculum

Teacher Knowledge

In this lesson the children will look at 'The Gleaners' by Millet (1857) to explore how painters use foreground, middle ground and background to create an illusion of depth. The painting shows three peasant women gleaning. This means that they were collecting the stray bits of wheat after the harvest, for their own use. The painting is famous for featuring the lower peasant class in a sympathetic way and as such was received poorly by the French upper classes, who, in the wake of the French Revolution were uneasy with such a depiction. The painting's large size, 84x112 cm, was another reason for its poor reception when it was first exhibited: large scale paintings were usually reserved for important historical or mythological paintings. The painting is an example of realism in art, both in the choice of subject matter and in its execution.

Knowledge Objective	Task	Lesson Detail	Vocabulary
To understand how artists use foreground, middle ground and background to create depth.	***Divergent Outcome*** *To draw the different layers of a landscape*	**Prior learning:** Look at the children's drawings of 3d shapes from last lesson. Ask: *Is the object 2d or 3d? What do I mean by 2d/3d? Does the object look 2d or 3d? How has the artist made the object look 3d?* **Vocabulary:** Read through Knowledge Objective and vocabulary. Remind the children that we are looking at space and today we will look at how the space between different objects in a picture can create an illusion of depth. **Look:** Show the children Millet's *The Gleaners* (1857). Ask: What can you see? Do you think the people in the painting look real? Why? Do they look 3d? Point out to the children that the women look 3d because of the different tones showing the curve of their arms, heads and bodies. Ask the children how many people they can see in the painting. Holding a pencil up to the picture and with their arm stretched out they should measure the biggest person they can see in the picture and then measure the smallest person they can see against the pencil. Ask: Why are the people different sizes? **Teach:** Explain that the people in the painting are different sizes because some are closer to us and some are further away. At the front the people are very large because they are closer to us. At the back the people are very small because they are further away. This is called foreshortening – go through term in knowledge organiser. Go through terms foreground, middle ground and background with knowledge organiser. Explain that artists will make objects larger and more detailed in the foreground to show that they are close to us and less detailed and smaller in the background to show they are further away from us. In this way artists create an illusion of depth of space in a painting. In particular, point out that in this painting in the foreground we can see individual blades of wheat, whereas in the background we cannot see such detail. Go through information shown in teacher knowledge above about the painting. **Demonstrate/Task:** Introduce the project that the children will develop for the rest of the unit: they will make landscapes using cardboard to make different layers (see examples in resources). In this lesson they will make initial sketches of different layers of landscapes from photographs (see resources for landscape photographs). In each of the photos ask the children to show you the foreground, middle ground and background. Explain to the children that today they will do line drawings to show the main shapes in the landscape and the different layers of the landscape. The children should start by doing 2 small scale sketches of the main shapes they see in the foreground, middle ground and background of two of the photographs (see resources for example sketches). The children should then pick which drawing they want to develop and create a larger version on A3 sugar paper. They should draw simple shapes using outlines only. **Partner teach/Plenary:** Children to reflect on their drawings. Ask: *What does foreground/middle ground/background mean? Show me the foreground/middle ground/background in your drawing.*	• foreground • background • middle ground • foreshortening
Knowledge Goals	**Skills Development**		**Relevant Artists**
Foreground means the part of the view that is closest to us in a picture and background means the part of the view that is furthest away from us in a picture Middle ground is between the foreground and the background Foreshortening means where an object is bigger in the foreground and smaller in the background	•Look carefully at the shapes of the main objects in the photographs •Hold the pencil in a firm but relaxed grip •Use the 2b pencil for drawing lines in your drawing •Draw lines to show the outside of the main shapes you can see in the photograph, do not draw detail inside the shapes •Draw shapes that you see in foreground, middle ground and background		Millet

Suggested Resources	2b pencils, sketchbooks, A3 sugar paper.

Figure 5.1 Lesson plan from the Primary Knowledge Curriculum for Year 4

This lesson plan, from the Primary Knowledge Curriculum for Year 4, shows key characteristics of a good art lesson. The lesson focus is on the visual element of 'space'. In the 'lesson detail' section we can see:

- Prior learning (retrieval practice).
- Vocabulary (explicit teaching of vocabulary).
- Look (questioning and discussion in response to a stimulus).
- Teach (explicit teaching of theoretical/disciplinary knowledge).
- Demonstrate/task (explicit teaching of practical knowledge and time to practise/create).
- Partner teach/plenary (retrieval practice and evaluation of pupil's work).

Retrieval practice

We have seen in Chapter 2 that we learn by connecting new knowledge with existing knowledge. Part of doing this successfully is starting by remembering what we already know: activating our prior knowledge. For this reason, retrieval practice is important at the beginning of every lesson. As well as activating prior knowledge it allows teachers to assess what pupils know and remember, and address any gaps in knowledge or misconceptions which may have arisen.

What can we do in art and design lessons to activate prior knowledge? What methods can we use? Merely going over information does not help pupils internalise it. It is active retrieval which strengthens the memory. Here are some ideas:

- Ask a question about a particular theoretical/practical/disciplinary concept which the pupils have previously learned about. For example, in Year 1, show children the primary colours and ask: *What is the name for these colours? Why are they special? What happens when we mix them together?*
- Show an artwork which relates to an element of art, an idea, a movement or a genre which the pupils have studied. Ask a question in relation to it, for example: *Who created this? Name the lines/colours/shapes which it uses. Describe how it uses line/colour/shape.*

- Present a multiple choice question which provides alternative answers for a particular definition for an element of art or a particular type of art like portraiture or landscape painting.
- Present a multiple choice question which provides alternative answers for characteristics of a genre/movement.
- Ask pupils to review the work they completed in a previous lesson. Ask them to describe the materials they used to create it and the different steps they took.

Reviewing what pupils have learned during the course of a lesson is also important. A plenary, at the end of a lesson, which gives pupils the opportunity to connect practical knowledge with theoretical and disciplinary knowledge deepens their understanding. A good example is shown in the plenary of the case study above: pupils are asked to reflect on their sketches and identify the foreground, middle ground and background in them. This allows them to evaluate the practical skill of observing shapes in a scene, drawing those shapes with a pencil and connecting these skills with theoretical/disciplinary knowledge about how artists can create space or depth in a picture.

Explicit teaching: vocabulary, theoretical and disciplinary knowledge

If we have a well-sequenced, specified curriculum which aims to incrementally increase pupils' knowledge and understanding we do this by explicitly teaching them what we want them to know. The idea of explicit teaching or instruction, however, is often misunderstood as meaning the teacher delivering a monologue from the front of the classroom. That tends to result in a group of pupils who are passive, bored and remember very little of what they have been told.

David Didau emphasises the importance of pupil participation: 'as participation falls, so does thinking, and with it meaning-making. For children to make meaning, they must *think*... Explanation without participation is the *opposite* of effective instruction' (Didau, 2025). He emphasises the importance of dialogue: fully guided instruction is 'structured interaction: teachers explain, model, question, check, and adapt in response to what students show they understand' (Didau, 2025).

How can we get teachers to achieve such structured interaction in art lessons? The following table makes some suggestions to share and practise with your team. They reflect some of the key findings from Rosenshine's research (2012), referred to in Chapter 2. The importance of explicit teaching in relation to practical skills, by way of modelling is discussed in Chapter 7.

Set clear learning objectives. Begin each lesson with the learning objective and communicate to pupils what they are going to learn. This helps them to see the purpose of what they are learning and guides their thinking.	**Explicitly introduce new key vocabulary.** Ask pupils to orally rehearse vocabulary at the beginning of a lesson at the same time as showing simple accompanying images and using actions. Share and discuss child-friendly definitions.
Provide new material (e.g. explaining an aspect of theoretical or disciplinary knowledge) **in small steps**. This allows pupil to grasp one piece of information before moving on to the next.	**Plan and ask questions** about the content of what you are teaching. Questioning promotes thinking and discussion and allows teachers to check what pupils understand and correct misconceptions.
Model answering questions using complete sentences and taught vocabulary. **Ask pupils to discuss their answers with each other** (partner talk). When they discuss their responses with each other they gain confidence and work out their ideas.	**Provide sentence starters** which pupils can use to aid their own answers. This provides a scaffold for pupils' conversation. **Ask pupils to share their responses with the class.** By explicitly teaching vocabulary, modelling, scaffolding and asking pupils to practise talking, prior to sharing with a larger group, all pupils should be able to contribute to class discussion.

Language, questioning and discussion

We have seen above how we can encourage teachers to structure teaching to aid thought and interaction. Part of this is planning for, and encouraging, discussion. Talking and language are, of course, foundational for children's development. Through talking, pupils express and form their ideas, thoughts and emotions. Talking and discussion, therefore, should be a central part of the art classroom.

We know that some children begin school having been exposed to a far greater breadth of vocabulary than others. Hart and Risley (2003) estimated this word gap (the number of words a child hears in their first four years of life) could be up to 30 million words. It's estimated that 69 per cent of primary school teachers have said the number of pupils with limited vocabulary is increasing in their schools compared to a few years ago (Oxford University Press, 2018).

Actively teaching vocabulary and the use of language in the classroom is, therefore, extremely important in ensuring that all pupils have equal access to education. We can specify key words that will be used in each art lesson and explicitly teach these at the beginning of the lesson. We can reinforce the meaning of words by breaking them down to identify their roots and etymology (for example, relating 'primary colours' to the etymology of the word 'primary' which comes from the Latin word *primus* meaning first). We can model how vocabulary is used in context and provide sentence stems to scaffold how to use the words in a complete sentence. Throughout the course of a lesson, we can then create opportunities for pupils to use and practise these words.

Encouraging discussion in the classroom is facilitated by asking questions. Effective questioning is one of the key characteristics of good teaching. It also allows teachers to check what pupils understand and correct misconceptions. What then, makes an effective question or series of questions? Part of this is understanding the purpose of the question that is being asked and using this to plan particular questions. The purpose of a question during the retrieval part of a lesson is to activate the memory of a particular piece of information. It will likely to be a closed question requiring a specific answer, for example: What are the secondary colours? In contrast, questions which promote deeper engagement, critical thinking and encourage dialogue between students are likely to be more open. Questions used when looking at and analysing and interpreting images are a case in point. These are discussed in Chapter 6.

Tasks and time to practise

An important part of each art lesson will be setting a task and giving pupils time to complete that task. Giving sufficient time to practise is what builds knowledge of different methods and techniques that are particular to different areas of making. Tasks should also develop the processes which are part of the practice of art and design: exploration and experimentation; invention, design and planning; and evaluation. These are discussed in Chapter 8.

The Ofsted research review (2023) emphasises the importance of understanding that tasks serve different purposes. There is the need for balance between pupils' learning established skills and using their own creative exploration referring to knowledge they have already acquired. Some will build towards convergent endpoints, where 'we are aware of how pupils will apply this information… for example, specific techniques to command a particular skill' (Ofsted, 2023). Others will build towards divergent outcomes 'where we do not know how pupils will use the knowledge…pupils draw on the knowledge to create their own artwork, combining what they know in sometimes experimental contexts...for example, the use of different media or visual cues can convey a personal style' (Ofsted, 2023).

A unit of work might require an approach where a pupil initially completes tasks following a step-by-step approach to reach a prescribed outcome, before using the skills they have learned for an expressive/experimental response in later lessons. A series of five lessons in a Year 2 unit on colour might look something like this:

- Lesson one – convergent task: revisiting a Year 1 task, practising mixing primary colours to make secondary colours, painting sheets of paper with primary or secondary colours, distinguishing which sheets are warm or cool colours.
- Lesson two – divergent task: using the sheets of paper painted in lesson one to create an abstract warm or cool collage using cut-out shapes.
- Lesson three – convergent task: practising mixing and painting tints and shades of blue so these get lighter and darker within a grid.
- Lesson four – divergent task: painting a splash of water using tints and shades of blue.
- Lesson five – divergent task: creating a rough seascape using mixed media of wax resist, tints and shades of blue paint washes, dilute black ink washes and graphite sticks.
- Lesson six – evaluating and reflecting on the work they have produced from lessons one to five.

Teaching art and design in EYFS

The EYFS statutory framework emphasises how children in Nursery and Reception learn very much through exploration, experimentation and play, and that part of a teacher's role is to stimulate their interest and respond to their emerging needs (DfE, 2025). This active learning where 'children have and develop their own ideas, make links between ideas, and develop strategies for doing things' means that teaching art and design in this age group is going to look different from how it looks in later key stages.

In EYFS it will sometimes be appropriate to show or tell children what to do through explicit teaching, for example, when they are learning something for the first time. This may be followed by opportunities for children to use and apply this new knowledge through play. At other times, it may be appropriate for children to explore something through play first and for the teacher to intervene with guidance at appropriate points. Making decisions in this way about how to teach is a key part of the teacher's role.

Example PD session: planning for explicit instruction

Here is an example PD session where teachers can think about planning for explicit instruction in an art lesson.

TIMING SUGGESTION	SESSION GUIDANCE
20 mins	• Read the blog 'Tom Sherrington's division of Rosenshine's principles of instruction into strands' (Beale, 2020) which summarises Rosenshine's principles of instruction. • Review the ten principles together as a group. • Explain that the teachers will use these to help plan explicit instruction for an art lesson.
20 mins	Ask teachers to choose a lesson they are about to teach and ask them to: • Write a clear learning objective. • Plan what retrieval questions they will ask. • Plan what key vocabulary they will introduce. • Decide what images/actions they will use to teach this. vocabulary and how they can break the words down. • Plan how they will break down new material into manageable chunks. • Write three questions which relate to the new material. • Write model answers and sentence starters for answers to these questions.
15 mins	Feedback, review and reflect on the planning the teachers have done as a group.

Chapter summary

- It is important that teachers have a clear plan about what core practical, theoretical and disciplinary knowledge they want pupils to learn in each lesson, and how this is specified and structured over a series of lessons.

- Key features that a good art lesson might include are: retrieval practice, explicit teaching of vocabulary, theoretical/disciplinary and practical knowledge, questioning and discussion in response to a stimulus, time to practise and create, and pupils' evaluation of their own work.
- Explicit instruction should incorporate structured interaction where pupils participate in discussion.
- Actively teaching vocabulary and the use of language in the classroom is important in ensuring that all pupils have equal access to education.
- An important part of each art lesson will be setting a task and giving pupils time to complete that task. There should be a balance in these tasks between pupils' learning established skills and using their own creative exploration.

Questions for reflection

Look at lesson plans and consider observations you have carried out as a part of your role.

- What core knowledge is specified in lesson plans?
- What features does each lesson incorporate?
- How do teachers plan for explicit instruction?
- How is vocabulary taught?
- What is the balance between convergent/divergent tasks set?

Explore further

- David Didau's blog about explicit instruction: www.daviddidau.substack.com/p/the-just-tell-them-trap
- Jonathan Beale's blog about Rosenshine's principles: www.cirl.etoncollege.com/tom-sherringtons-division-of-rosenshines-principles-of-instruction-into-strands

6 Time to look

In this chapter, we will explore why the skill of 'looking' is important in art and design.

The National Curriculum for England for Key Stage 1 and 2 requires us to ensure not only that pupils acquire knowledge and skills to be able to create art but also to 'think critically and develop a more rigorous understanding of art and design' and 'know how art and design both reflect and shape our history, and contribute to the culture, creativity and wealth of our nation' (DfE, 2013).

Pupils learn by making connections between other peoples' art which they encounter, and art which they create themselves. Teaching them the art of looking will help to develop their understanding of what they see. As subject leaders we need to ensure that teachers understand how to develop pupil's skills in looking.

In this chapter we will consider:

- what we mean by 'looking'
- the importance of 'visual literacy'
- looking in the primary classroom
- looking and thinking
- looking and drawing
- looking and talking.

What do we mean by 'looking' and 'visual literacy'?

We might think that looking is not a skill which requires much direction. Don't we use our eyes in every waking moment to see, assess and make decisions to guide very effectively what we do? In fact, careful observation or looking closely is a key skill which many artists say forms the basis of what they do. The Canadian photographer Freeman Patterson wrote: 'Seeing, in the finest and broadest sense, means using your senses, your intellect, and your emotions...

It means looking beyond the labels of things and discovering the remarkable world around you' (2011).

Looking closely then, or careful observation, does not mean a cursory glance: it suggests a depth of engagement with what pupils see which demands analysis and critical thinking. It develops their powers of perception, not only allowing them to see what is in the world around them, but to build on their understanding of what they see. Once they understand it better, they can then communicate what they think about it. Teachers can pair asking pupils to look closely with learning specialist vocabulary and opportunities for discussion. In this way pupils will become more fluent in their expression of ideas: careful observation can become the cornerstone for sophisticated debate in the art classroom.

The act of practising careful observation is sometimes referred to as 'visual literacy'. Visual literacy has been described as 'the ability to interpret, understand and create visual content effectively. It involves recognising and analysing visual elements... to communicate and comprehend information' (Art UK, 2025). Barnes, an artist and lecturer, identifies the importance of this skill for young children, so that they can understand the world around them (2015).

The importance of visual literacy

In a multimedia age, so saturated with images, being visually literate is something which seems more important than ever. Pupils are bombarded with images every day: on phones, computers, televisions, in shop windows, bus stops and train platforms. The sheer volume of these images requires them to engage with and interpret what they see at break-neck speed. We live in the age of constant visual stimulation and yet seem only to glance.

Concerns about a lack of teaching of art in primary schools and the development of pupils' visual literacy in particular have driven research and the development of resources particularly aimed at primary schools.[1] Katie Leonard, the head of learning at Art UK, which has developed an online looking resource for primary schools, refers to visual literacy as the 'missing pillar of primary education'. She makes the case for developing visual literacy in schools

[1] In November 2024 the Education Department of Oxford University launched a three year study to measure how the observation and discussion of works of art in schools can support the development of visual literacy and communication skills in students (www.education.ox.ac.uk/news/visual-literacy-research-launched-to-assess-how-looking-at-art-can-impact-young-peoples-future-success). The 'Superpower of Looking' is a primary resource promoted by Art UK: www.artuk.org/learn/the-superpower-of-looking.

asserting that it can enhance retention, critical thinking and communication and build emotional, social and cultural understanding (Leonard, 2024). Let's look at each of these benefits in turn.

1. Engaging with images in the classroom can enhance retention. Using images can make information more accessible and more memorable to pupils. Where images are combined with words we call this dual coding. Dual coding theory is the idea that information is more effectively learned and remembered when presented in two formats, verbal (spoken or written words), and non-verbal (images, diagrams or symbols).
2. Engaging with images promotes critical thinking. This means making reasoned judgements on the basis of interpreting, understanding, synthesising and applying information (Burns and Sinfield, 2016). In art this entails discussing *what* we see, *how* what we see is communicated and what *meaning* and *purpose* if any, lies behind it. The act of such discussion, using subject specific vocabulary which has been explicitly taught, develops a pupil's communication skills.
3. Looking at and talking about art from a broad range of cultures, genres and across time builds pupils' emotional, social and cultural understanding. As such, looking at a broad range of art is an inclusive activity. It involves open enquiry and allows anyone who looks to have a voice. Looking opens up art to *all* children in the classroom, rather than just those whose parents might take them to a gallery or museum. Giving children regular opportunities to express their views about what they see can boost their confidence. Combining this with teaching subject-specific vocabulary and contextual information about what they see, empowers children to engage with the visual world in a critical manner.

Looking in the primary art classroom

Now we've seen that careful looking fosters retention, critical thinking, communication and builds emotional, social and cultural understanding, what does it look like in the primary classroom? Actively employing looking in the classroom emphasises the value of the looking process. As subject leads how can we ensure that active looking is used in our schools, from EYFS to Year 6? How can we ensure that pupils understand and become curious about the rich world of art that exists all around us, talk about what they see and use that work as inspiration to drive and inform their own creative responses?

Looking is such a vital part of the process of understanding visual art that we might well consider that it should form a discrete part of every art lesson, from EYFS to Year 6. Such activities pair looking with giving pupils the time to think, time to draw and time to talk. The following paragraphs set out examples of looking activities, which you as subject lead can encourage teachers to use as part of their art lessons.

Looking and thinking

In her book about learning mathematics, Jo Boaler debunks the idea that learning maths is not about speed but is rather about thinking carefully and making connections (2009). This proposition applies with equal force to art. There is a tendency in schools generally for teachers to focus on speed of response as evidence of fast thinking and as a mark of success. However, fast *looking* can mean that pupils engage with what they are looking at in a cursory or superficial way. Giving pupils time to look slowly and consider an image *before* speaking about it encourages them to explore an image more thoroughly with their eyes.

Here are some different activities which can be used successfully used from EYFS to Key Stage 2 to give children time to ponder and undertake this exploration. In each case allow the pupils to think about the question which has been posed and look for at least 30 seconds.

- Ask pupils to imagine they have jumped into the picture. Ask them to think about what they can *see* and how they *feel*.
- Ask younger pupils to think of three things they notice in the picture. Ask older pupils to write down a list of ten things they notice.
- Ask pupils to think about which part of the picture they want to look at most, or which part their eye is most drawn to and why.
- Ask pupils to think of a question they have about what they can see.
- Ask younger pupils to think of three words which the picture makes them think of. Ask older pupils to write down five words which the picture makes them think of.
- Create a reproduction of the image and cut it up into pieces so it resembles a jigsaw puzzle. In groups, ask the pupils to put the jigsaw together.

Looking and drawing

When we draw we look more intensely than we ordinarily might do. It is obvious that observing closely is necessary for drawing. What is not so obvious, however, is that drawing itself can be used as a vehicle for seeing or observing more closely. Careful looking is necessary to facilitate drawing, and drawing can enable us to see more clearly.

The process of looking for the purposes of drawing makes us observe more deeply than we otherwise would. If we are drawing from our observation of an object, scene or image in front of us we necessarily have to look at that object, scene or image to observe the lines, shapes, colours and forms which make up the detail of what we see. Our eyes pass frequently from the object, scene or image to the paper. As we look, with the objective of recreating what we see in front of us we begin to engage in more detail with what we see, to notice things that we had not noticed before, and to perceive what we are seeing in different ways. People often say that the process of drawing a scene in front of them means that they can easily recall that scene in their mind's eye. It is as if the process of looking hard to enable drawing etches the scene in our memory.

In the primary classroom we can use various looking and drawing 'techniques' which enable pupils to look more closely. This may be a vehicle for getting to know an existing image more thoroughly or it may occur in the process of producing a drawing of real objects or a scene. Some suggested techniques are listed below.

- **Look at the width and height of what you are going to draw before starting to draw**. Consider whether the paper should be wide (i.e. in landscape format) or tall (i.e. in portrait format).
- **Use a viewfinder to find the edges of your view.** A viewfinder can be made very simply by cutting a rectangular hole in a piece of paper.
- **With a finger, trace lines/shapes in the air before creating these lines/ shapes on the paper.** This might mean rehearsing the outside shape of an object such as a pear.
- **Find important points in the image/view and with small marks indicate where these will go on the page.** This might be the top of a person's head or their feet, the edge of a table or a horizon line.
- **Measure the relative size of different objects in the image/view with a pencil.** Hold the pencil in the air vertically with a straight arm (this will mean that the relative measurements are consistent) and cover one eye.

Place the top of the pencil against the top of the object you want to draw and observe how far the bottom of the object comes down the pencil. Compare with another object in the image/view.

- **Screw up your eyes (squint) to look at a scene/group of objects.** This has the effect of making it easier to identify where the scene/group of objects appears to be very dark or very light. This is a useful exercise when creating tonal drawing, for example, with chalk and charcoal. Identify where you can see the lightest light and the darkest dark.
- **Lightly sketch the outside of large shapes in your image/view.** Be aware that in reality some shapes may sit behind or in front of other shapes. Be aware that lightly sketched large shapes can also include the outside shape of cast shadows or blocks of colour.
- **Identify and lightly sketch the spaces between objects rather than object themselves.** This is called negative space.

The following three drawing tasks use some of the techniques specified above.

In practice: creating quick drawings to get to know a piece of art

This three or four-stage task can be used successfully with pupils from Year 2 upwards.

Show the pupils Figure 6.1: Hobbema's painting *The Avenue at Middelharnis* (1689, The National Gallery, London) which is a famous Dutch landscape painting. It shows a road leading to a village in South Holland, in the Netherlands. It is known for its unusual symmetrical composition.

Ask the pupils to copy the picture using just lines to indicate the different shapes and lines which can be seen in the painting. Before they start drawing, ask them to consider the width and height of the image and whether they should use the paper in landscape or portrait format. Then, ask them to trace the shape of the receding road in the air with their finger.

Ask them to produce three different drawings in accordance with the instructions below (for examples of each drawing see Figure 6.2). Spend two minutes on each drawing.

- **Drawing one:** Copy the lines and shapes that you see in the painting.
- **Drawing two:** Copy the lines and shapes that you see in the painting, but once you start drawing try not to take your pencil off the page. This is a

continuous line drawing. (This method means that there are connecting lines between the different shapes which you draw. It will make the drawing more fluid in style.)

- **Drawing three:** Copy the painting for a final time using lines and shapes as in 'drawing 1', but this time use your non-dominant hand. (Again, this produces a drawing of increased fluidity and ensures that pupils lose their self-consciousness about what the drawing looks like in the end: their focus in on the process of looking rather than the drawing as a finished product.)

This series of three drawings is a good technique to employ with many paintings. It allows pupils to become more familiar with an image. To extend the activity add a fourth drawing to be completed with a partner:

- **Drawing four:** Place a piece of paper on a clip board. One person should hold the board with their back to the painting. The other person should hold a pencil. They need to draw the image by holding the pencil tip on the board and asking the person who is holding the board to move it to create lines and shapes which resemble the painting.

Figure 6.1 Hobbema, M. (1689), *The Avenue at Middelharnis* [oil on canvas], The National Gallery, London

Figure 6.2 Year 2 responses to The Avenue at Middelharnis

In practice: drawing a still life using cross-hatching

This task can be used successfully with pupils from Year 3 upwards.

Set up at least six or seven still life objects in the middle of the room on top of a piece of cloth. Pupils should sit around the still life so they can all see it from different angles. Ideally have small boxes under the material to provide a variety of levels which the objects can sit on. Avoid glass objects as transparency is difficult to draw, and anything with writing on it, as this will distract the pupils from the form of the objects. Objects such as wooden boxes, opaque bottles (or dark glass), cups and bowls are generally successful. If spot lighting is available to shine from one angle, then use this as it will make the different tones on the object more obvious. However, if this is not available switch off electrical lighting and rely on natural light from the window. (A wash of electrical lighting tends to flatten the tonal variation and makes the forms more difficult to read.)

- **Ask the pupils to start by looking:** They are going to draw what they see, not what they think they see. They will not be able to see the whole of each object as some objects will obscure parts of other objects. Encourage them to squint to see darks and lights more clearly. Before they start drawing ask them to consider the width and height of the whole group of objects. and whether they should use the paper in landscape or portrait format. Ask: Where is the biggest/smallest object? Where does the light fall? Where is the lightest part/darkest part?
- **Ask the pupils to find the largest object they can see and draw the shape of the object in the air with their finger.** Do the same with the smallest object.
- **Ask the pupils to use a pencil to lightly sketch the outline of the different shapes of the objects AND the shapes of the cast shadows which fall underneath them.** Ask: What different lines (e.g. straight, curved) will you need to use? They should make the objects fill the paper they are working on.
- **Next, ask the pupils to pick one object to add cross-hatching to.** Ask: How will you use cross-hatching to vary the tone? Point out that they should use stronger lines closer together for darker areas, and light lines further apart for lighter tones. They should draw the lines loosely, so the cross-hatching doesn't look like a grid. Ask them to practise a dark, mid and light area of cross-hatching on the side of the paper before they start using it on an object.

Figure 6.3 Year 3 cross-hatched still life drawing

In practice: creating quick figure drawings of an artist's mannequin

This task can be used successfully with pupils from Year 1 upwards.

- Ask the pupils to think of one of the games they play in the playground. Ask a pupil to hold their body in a freeze-frame as if they are in the middle of playing the game (e.g. kicking a football).
- Show the pupils how to put an artist's mannequin in the same position and then ask a pupil to do this. They should think about the position of the head, arms, hands, body, legs and feet.
- The pupils then have one minute to draw the mannequin. At first ask them to look carefully at the mannequin concentrating on the position of their arms and legs. Ask: Are they standing on one leg? Are their arms raised?
- Ask them to put a mark somewhere near the top of the paper to show the top of the head. Then ask them to put two marks somewhere near the bottom of the paper to show where the two feet will go.
- Then draw single lines to show the direction of the different parts of the body, so they end up with a stick person.
- Then, add the shapes of the different parts of the arms, legs, body and head.
- Repeat the exercise multiple times so each pupil has multiple figures on their page.

Figure 6.4 Year 1 figure drawings

Looking and talking

Getting pupils to talk about what they see is a powerful vehicle for improving their skills in thinking critically about what they observe. By talking, we can develop and hone our ideas about the visual world we encounter. When given regular opportunities to discuss a range of art in the classroom pupils grow in confidence to express their thoughts with fluency. It also gives them agency to engage with the 'art world'. Galleries, museums, exhibitions, documentaries, articles in magazines, newspapers and blogs need not feel like a closed shop to a child who has looked hard, learned about what they have seen and discussed it with their peers.

Talking about what we see starts with careful looking. The suggested approaches to looking and thinking in the section on page 76 can be used *before* pupils verbally articulate what they think about what they see.

As teachers, our questioning skills are our tools for facilitating looking. Asking appropriate questions enables pupils to critically observe, analyse, question and interpret the images we put before them. When we ask open questions, before we give too much information about an image, this allows a pupil to look openly with a spirit of enquiry. For example: 'What can you see in the picture?'. When followed by specific questions that direct a mode of enquiry or respond to something particular a pupil has said, we promote slow and careful looking. Giving too much information too early tends to shut down enquiry and stunt their willingness to explore with their eyes. After they have explored the image by looking, we can then give them more information, by way of direct instruction about what they see. This approach is demonstrated when looking at the Monet image on page 85.

If we are promoting a spirit of open enquiry by looking, it is important that in our responses to children's observations, we do not facilitate misconceptions. For example, a child might say that in an abstract painting they can identity a shape which reminds them of an elephant and then proceed on the basis that the painting is definitely a representation of an elephant rather than an abstract painting which does not seek to represent reality. If we do not redirect the mistaken notion we would be facilitating a misconception. One way of preventing a classroom discussion proceeding on a tangent and creating misconceptions is to ask pupils for evidence about what they say they can see. This approach is also demonstrated in the case study on page 88 by way of follow-up questions which probe why pupils have said what they say about what they can see. In other words, what evidence can they show from the image which supports what they have said.

Here are some different questioning structures, using open questions, which can be useful to get pupils talking about what they see when initially encountering an image.

- Ask: What can you see? What do you know? What can you guess?
- Ask: What can you see? Where is it? Who is in it? When is it? Why do you think the artwork has been made?
- Isolate different parts of an image and ask: What can you see? What do you think the rest of the image shows?
- Ask: What does the picture make you imagine?
- Ask: What questions do you have about the picture?
- Compare two images and ask: What is different? What is similar?
- Ask questions which relate to the elements of art which make up a design: What can you say about the colour/line/shape/form/tone/space/texture shown in this image?
- After completing a drawing copying an image (see 'In practice' on page 85) ask: Is there anything which you have spotted which you didn't notice at first?

All of these questions can be a springboard for class conversation about an image. Coupled with specific and directed follow-up questions which focus on what is relevant to a particular image, scaffolds such as sentence starters and clear modelling of talk (which utilises appropriate subject specific vocabulary), children will develop their skills and confidence in looking critically, making inferences and speaking about art.

Explicitly teaching and revising subject-specific and relevant vocabulary at the beginning of a lesson, providing sentence starters and clearly modelling complete sentences will give pupils the best possible assistance in talking articulately in response to questions about what they see. This area is covered more fully in Chapter 5 on vocabulary. Some suggested sentence starters are shown below:

- 'The picture makes me feel… because…'
- 'The brushstrokes suggest that… because…'
- 'The colours are… which suggests…'
- 'I can see… lines which show me that…'

At Key Stage 2, pupils can begin to write down their observations by way of annotation around an image, in note form (maybe two or three bullet points and a short phrase per question) to articulate their initial observations about an image.

In practice: annotating an image

Show the pupils *The Beach at Trouville* by Monet (1870, The National Gallery, London). Ask them to do three different drawings of the painting in the manner of the Hobbema task detailed on page 78. They should take two minutes to do each drawing.

Ask them to annotate a small copy of the painting using bullet points and short phrases to say: What can you see? Where is it? Who is in it? When is it? Why do you think the artwork has been made?

See below for examples of likely answers followed by more directed/specific follow-up questions in italics for discussion:

What can you see?

- Two ladies on a beach. *How do you know they are on a beach?*
- Two women holding umbrellas. *Why do you think they are holding umbrellas?*
- Two women dressed in old-fashioned clothes. *What is old fashioned about what they are wearing? What is behind them?*
- Two ladies sitting on a beach in the bright sunshine. *How do you know it is sunny? What colour is the sky?*
- Two women and a chair. *Is it the kind of chair you might take to the beach?*

Where is it?

- On a beach. *How do you know it is a beach?*
- Outside. *How do you know they are outside? Why would they have chairs outside?*

Who is in it?

- Two women from olden times. *Why do you think they are from olden times? Can you see the whole of each woman? Can you see the features on their faces?*
- Two women holding umbrellas and wearing hats. *Do you think it is raining? If not, why do you think they are holding up umbrellas?*

When is it?

- A long time ago. *Why do you think this painting isn't showing the present day?*
- During the day. *How do you know?*
- In the summer. *What in the picture shows you it is summertime?*

Why do you think the artwork has been made?

- To show what it's like on a beach. *How do you think the artist has made this picture?*
- To show a pretty beach scene. *Where do you think the artist was when they made this picture?*

After the pupils have completed the looking task give them some information about the painting. Specialist vocabulary which the pupils should be introduced to (see Chapter 5on teaching vocabulary) is indicated in bold type.

- **This is an impressionist painting by the painter Monet. Impressionism** was an art movement which developed in nineteenth-century France. It is partly known for paintings made outside, rather than in the **studio**. Main Impressionist subjects were **landscapes** and scenes from everyday life. This way of painting was new – up until this point artists had generally painted grander subjects, like battle-scenes, scenes from classical myths or grand portraits of rich people. It is partly known for paintings made outside, rather than in the **studio.**
- **This painting was painted outside (*en plein air*).** It is of two women on a beach in Northern France – one of them is Monet's wife. Monet and his wife were on their honeymoon. We can tell the painting was painted on the beach because there are grains of sand in the paint. It is a small painting (38 cm x 46.5 cm): keeping a painting small makes it easier to paint ***en plein air***. Impressionist painters had started to use paints from tubes which was a new technique. Before these were available, painters would have to grind up and mix pigments which would have been very hard to do outside.
- **This painting uses rapid brushwork.** It looks like the painting has been done quickly (also necessary when the weather changes rapidly outside) as there is little detail but broad **brushstrokes** of thick paint. We can actually see the **brushstrokes**. The painting shows **transient effects** of the weather. The

Impressionists wanted to capture, for instance, the way the light of the sun falls at a particular moment. Here we can see little detail on the women's faces, and strong contrasts of colour on their clothes to show bright light and shadow.

- **This is a scene of everyday life.** It is almost like a snapshot that we might take with a camera on the beach on holiday today. We can only see half of the body of the woman dressed in black.

Case study: ensuring that looking is taking place in the classroom

Sarah is an art leader in a two-form-entry school in Oxfordshire. This is her second year in the role and, having ensured that art lessons are taking place each week she wants to guarantee that there are looking activities happening in all art lessons.

Sarah starts by looking at lesson plans for each year group to see if she can identify looking activities taking part in any of the lessons which have been planned. She also observes a lesson in each year group to see what looking activities she can identify in the classroom.

She finds that in many of the lessons that are planned/taking place the pupils are asked to look at a piece of artwork, very briefly before the teacher tells them something about it. The pupils seem anxious in each lesson to get on with their practical art-making rather than engaging with the art which they are being asked to look at.

Sarah plans and leads a staff meeting for teachers to ensure that they understand the importance of looking in the art classroom. This incorporates sample looking activities involving thinking, drawing and talking.

She uses her subject leader time over the course of the next month to model teach a lesson in each key stage incorporating a looking task in each lesson.

She asks each year group to plan questions and follow-up questions to promote careful looking which they will ask in relation to each artwork which the pupils will look at in the next unit.

Example PD session: comparing two images

Here is an example of what a PD session on looking and questioning techniques comparing two images could look like. By completing the activity with their colleagues, teachers are encouraged to step into their pupil's shoes and develop their own understanding of how to build pupil's looking and communication skills. The activity can form the basis of a lesson. Teachers from Year 5 or 6 can use the initial open questions and follow-up questions to develop a lesson around these two images. Teachers from other year groups can develop a similar lesson comparing two other related images.

TIMING SUGGESTION	SESSION GUIDANCE
10 mins	Ask teachers to annotate *Migrant Mother* by Dorothea Lange (1936, Museum of Modern Art, New York) and *Glass Tears* by Man Ray (1932, The Getty Museum, Los Angeles) with bullet points in note form to say: • **what they can see** • **what is different** • **what is similar.**
2 mins	Ask teachers to read the information about the two photographs . • **Both of these photographs were taken in the 1930s.** They are very different from each other and show how photography was beginning to be used in very different ways in this period. • **Dorothea Lange was known as a pioneer of documentary photography.** This photograph was taken in the USA during the Great Depression, a time of great poverty, caused by an extreme economic downturn in the US. She took this photograph while employed by the US government to raise awareness of the plight of poor farmers. The photograph was published in magazines and newspapers and became a symbol of the poverty that existed. It is photography which aimed to record reality. • **Man Ray's photograph, taken only four years before Lange's is very different.** He was from the USA but spent much of his career in Paris, where he was primarily known as a painter but was also a photographer. At the time, the role of photography was much debated – it was questioned whether photography was something that could be more than just a medium for showing reality. For Man Ray, photography became an important means of artistic expression. This photograph is highly staged and carefully set up: the artist using glass beads to show the woman's tears. Note how it is taken close-up, and from an unusual angle.
10 mins	Ask teachers to write follow-up questions based on another teacher's annotated observations.

Chapter summary

- By teaching pupils the art of looking, we can help them to develop their understanding and interpretation of what they see.
- Looking carefully, being curious and interpreting what we see seems more important than ever in today's world. It is an activity which develops critical thinking and communication skills.
- In conjunction with thinking, drawing and talking, looking is a skill which we can teach through various activities in the classroom and make an important part of art lessons.
- Ensuring that looking activities are taking place in lessons regularly, allowing pupils to develop the skill of looking, is an important part of being a subject lead.

Questions for reflection

- What is the benefit to pupils of looking carefully, in art lessons or more generally?
- How will I ensure that staff understand the importance of looking in art?
- What opportunities for careful looking already exist in my school setting?
- How can I help teachers across the school to embed looking as a part of each art lesson? What looking activities will they use?

Explore further

- 'Superpower of Looking' Art UK primary resource: www.artuk.org/learn/the-superpower-of-looking
- Education Department of Oxford University study to measure how the observation and discussion of works of art in schools can support the development of visual literacy and communication skills in students: www.education.ox.ac.uk/news/visual-literacy-research-launched-to-assess-how-looking-at-art-can-impact-young-peoples-future-success
- The Tate Gallery guide to slow looking: https://www.tate.org.uk/art/guide-slow-looking

7 Guiding practice

A large part of teaching art and design is about guiding pupils in how to make art. Having a coherently sequenced curriculum is vital so that pupils have the opportunity to revisit knowledge and build skills previously acquired. If such a curriculum is in place, how do teachers in the classroom best teach pupils to develop their skills? How, as subject leads, do we ensure that our teachers are equipped to do this? What is best practice?

The Ofsted research review (2023) pinpoints how, to be able to make progress, pupils need:

- techniques modelled
- the opportunity to practise
- to receive timely feedback.

This chapter addresses how subject leads can facilitate teachers to do this looking at:

- building teacher confidence
- explicit teaching of skills (modelling)
- other scaffolds to help pupils develop art skills
- providing feedback.

Building teacher confidence

Many teachers lack confidence in their own artistic skills. This can be a barrier to effective teaching. At worst, it can cause a teacher to teach the practical part of a lesson in a cursory way or even to skip over it. It may also be interpreted as implying lack of interest or value in the subject itself.

In practice: practical suggestions for increasing teacher confidence

As a subject lead you can actively increase teacher confidence in a number of ways:

- Identify areas where teachers need help by talking to teachers and through subject monitoring.
- Provide professional development sessions which allow teachers to practise key artistic skills.
- Provide professional development sessions which allow teachers to practise explicit modelling of skills.
- Focus on a teacher's modelling of tasks in lesson observations/coaching sessions.
- Encourage teachers to practise modelling tasks in advance of teaching them in the classroom.

Explicit teaching of skills: modelling

Good teachers explicitly teach what students need to know. Rosenshine's research (2012) found that good teachers:

- present new material in small steps
- provide models
- provide scaffolds.

Employing these techniques, which are explored below, ensures that pupils are not overloaded with too much new information at once and can learn effectively.

In art, some of what we need to explicitly instruct pupils to do is to use materials effectively. Part of this can be achieved by teachers modelling or demonstrating to their pupils what to do.

Modelling

Demonstrating what pupils are going to do in the performance of a task allows pupils to see, step by step, how to carry out the task, and provides them with a model (or example) to work from. It is important that modelling different skills, and giving pupils the opportunity to practise those skills, forms an integral part of each lesson. Make sure that teachers in your school know that this is the expectation.

As subject leads, we can ensure that teachers are confident in modelling skills in art by providing professional development sessions. We can also make it the expectation that teachers always practise modelling before a lesson, so that they ensure they can do it clearly, are aware of the key points they need to get across and discover any difficulties or pitfalls before showing the pupils what to do. Such practise need only take a few minutes in advance of a lesson.

Desktop visualisers are a good tool in the classroom as they allow a teacher to model to a whole class, so that each individual pupil can see. They are particularly good when showing pupils something close up, for example, how to thread a needle or load a brush. Be aware that they will not always be appropriate, for example, when demonstrating something on a large scale.

Here are five key things for teachers to remember to ensure that they are modelling effectively:

- **Use the same resources that the pupils will use.** Pupils need to see how the materials behave. This will not be clear if, for example, a pencil on paper is substituted with a marker on a whiteboard.
- **Break the task down into manageable steps**. In a painting task this might consist of (1) mixing the paint, (2) loading the brush, (3) applying the paint to the paper.
- **Be specific.** Think about the details that the pupils need to know to be able to succeed. For example: Which way round should the paper be? Will they use the end or the side of an oil pastel? Do they need to press hard or lightly with their pencil?
- **Summarise**. Before the children start the task themselves, summarise the different steps they should take, either verbally or in succinct written bullet points.
- **Time**. Do not model for too long. Four to five minutes should enable pupils to gain an idea about what they need to do without overloading their working memory so that they stop paying attention.

In addition to these key points, encourage teachers to think aloud or narrate as they model. Demonstrating the thought process involved in tackling a particular task provides pupils with a clear approach to a task.

As we have seen in Chapter 2, the interplay between practical, theoretical and disciplinary knowledge in art is important in cementing pupils' understanding across the discipline (Ofsted, 2023). 'Thinking aloud' whilst demonstrating a practical task can also allow teachers to embed the connections pupils make between these different areas of knowledge.

In practice: 'thinking aloud' whilst modelling

A teacher demonstrating painting a rough seascape to Year 1 might talk about the following connections between different areas of knowledge while demonstrating what to do:

- We are using Monet's dramatic pictures of the sea to inspire our paintings (for example, see *The Sea at Fecamp*, 1881). What colours does Monet use to paint the sea and the sky?
- Just like Monet, we are going to use tints and shades of blue. How do we make tints and shades? How are we going to mix our tints and shades successfully?
- How can you describe the difference between how Monet paints the sea and the sky? Describe the brushstrokes he has used.
- How can we use our brush to create a rough sea? How will our brushstrokes in the sea and the sky be different? What effect does using different types of brushstroke have?

Lesson plans

As subject leads we can emphasise the importance of modelling by expressly stipulating that it should be included as a part of each lesson plan. Lesson plans can specify the keys points which a teacher needs to communicate to pupils when demonstrating a particular task. This is particularly helpful as a checklist for teachers who lack confidence in their own skills.

Key points for teaching a Reception or Year 1 class in the first stages of how to use a brush could include:

- Hold the brush like a pencil to give good control.
- Control the amount of water/paint that is loaded onto the brush.
- Mix colours thoroughly in the mixing palette.
- Wash the brush before loading it with a new colour.
- Pull the brush smoothly.

Modelling divergent outcomes and experimentation

The product of live modelling by the teacher in the classroom will of course provide an example for pupils to work from. Making this available for pupils to look at as they work can be advantageous. Especially where the expectation is that they are practising skills to produce broadly similar outcomes which have little variation across a class (convergent outcomes).

Within a carefully sequenced curriculum tasks should build so that, over time, pupils practise skills with increasing independence. In addition, an important process in the production of art is experimentation, where pupils apply techniques they have learned with undetermined endpoints (divergent outcomes).

If pupils are expected to work more independently, using skills previously acquired to experiment and produce varied outcomes, should teachers still model what to do? The danger of demonstrating a step-by-step process and then leaving this for pupils to look at as they complete their own work, is that it can stifle experimentation. They will often copy what the teacher has done even if they are told explicitly not to. However, many pupils, will find it challenging to experiment without being given guidance first.

Teachers need to consider the purpose of their demonstration. Rather than exploring a step-by-step process to demonstrate a prescribed skill, teachers are illustrating a range of possibilities which are a starting point for a child's imagination to flourish and in which they can apply their learning. It is helpful here, to set parameters which relate to what pupils have been learning about (for example, around shape, colour or materials) and show pupils a suggested range of approaches within those parameters.

In practice: modelling divergent outcomes/experimentation for Year 5

In the context of learning about the abstract expressionists who sought to convey emotion in abstract works (for example, Jackson Pollock or Alma Thomas) ask pupils to paint an abstract piece of work on thick multimedia paper using acrylic paint. Pupils should consider colour theory (warm or cool colours, analogous colours and complementary colours) and the effect of different lines, shapes, textures and use of space in the paintings they look at, before they start to paint.

As the teacher models their own response to the task they can ask questions to guide the pupils to consider the approach they will take:

- Will you alter the shape/dimensions of the paper you are working on by cutting it or will you use it as it is? Which way round do you want your paper?
- Will you plan the lines/shapes/colours you want on the paper by marking these on with a pencil or will you work intuitively with the paint, without planning beforehand?
- What mood do you want your picture to convey? How will you achieve this? What lines/shapes/colours/textures will you use?
- How will your colours work together? Will you choose warm or cool colours? If you choose colours which are next to each other on the colour wheel (analogous colours) how will this be different if you choose colours which are opposite each other (complementary colours)?
- How much space will there be between the shapes/lines in your painting? What effect will this have?
- How will you apply the paint? Will you use a brush/sponge/cloth? Do you want to show texture or a have a smooth surface? What effect will this have?

Summarise on a white board what the pupils need to think about as they work on their painting. For example:

- paper/plan
- mood
- colour
- line/shape
- texture
- tools.

Modelling and working towards independence

Modelling is a kind of scaffold. Other types of scaffold applicable to art are discussed on pages 98–99. A scaffold is a tool which supports pupils to achieve an intended outcome. A scaffold is a temporary support: it should be removed when it is no longer needed, when pupils are able to achieve the outcome independently.

By modelling, teachers provide information in small steps to help pupils learn a particular technique or skill. A carefully structured curriculum providing opportunities for practice will allow children to gradually work towards greater independence in the practice of their skills. This means that a teacher may model particular colour mixing techniques in Key Stage 1 which they do not then need to explicitly model to a pupil in upper Key Stage 2. The older pupil will be able to use and apply their colour mixing skills independently. It is at this point that a different kind of modelling is likely to be more appropriate, which presents pupils with a range of possibilities which are a starting point for a more open-ended task.

Modelling sketchbook use

Chapter 8 explores how sketchbooks are a place for exploratory work. They should act as working, developing documents which are a record of a pupil's thinking and artistic development. As such, it is tempting to think that pupils should use them 'freely' without particular guidance. However, if sketchbooks are going to be an integral and meaningful reflection of how pupils work, and what they have learned to do, they need to be explicitly shown how to use them.

It is effective if teachers and other adults in the classroom keep their own sketchbooks which can act as a cumulative model for pupils to work from. Subject leads can ensure that it is the expectation that this is part of what teachers do when teaching art. Where appropriate, teachers can model in their own sketchbooks.

Key considerations when modelling in sketchbooks might include:

- Is this work something which is appropriate for a sketchbook, i.e. exploratory work, including drawings, paintings, collage, exercises, cuttings, annotations and written reflections?
- What kind of task is the teacher modelling (i.e. convergent task/exercise or divergent/exploratory task)? How will this affect how they model the task?
- How will the work be presented? Which way round should the sketchbook be? How big will their work be? Do they want to use the whole page or compartmentalise a page so they can include different images on the same page?
- Do they want to date or title their work?
- How will the materials they are using affect how they use the sketchbook?
- When annotating an image or writing reflections on their own work should they write in full sentences or use note-form?

Example PD session: practising modelling

Here is an example of what a PD session might look like where teachers can practise modelling.

TIMING SUGGESTION	SESSION GUIDANCE
5 mins	• Remind teachers about the importance of modelling. Modelling should be part of every art lesson whether pupils are learning/practising particular skills or experimenting/using established skills to work with increasing independence. • Explain that by modelling, teachers are implementing good practice as identified in Rosenshine's research. Modelling is a type of scaffolding: a tool which supports learners to achieve an outcome. By modelling, teachers will be providing information in small steps and a guide for pupils to work from.

10 mins	• Explain that there are five key things to think about when modelling in art:
	  • using the same resources that the pupils will use
	  • breaking the task down into manageable steps
	  • being specific
	  • summarising
	  • time – taking four to five minutes to model a task.
	• Using a visualiser, model a KS1 task, highlighting the five key points above.

15 mins	• Working in pairs, grouped by key stage, ask teachers to model a task they will be teaching over the course of the next few weeks to each other. • As each teacher models, ask them to think about addressing the five key points. • After modelling ask the teacher watching to provide feedback to the teacher they have watched. Ask them to identify two points of good practice and one point for development. • Explain that the points of good practice and point for development will form part of the focus for forthcoming lesson observations.

Other scaffolds

Rosenshine's research (2012) found that good teachers provide scaffolds. A teacher provides scaffolding to ensure a pupil can successfully complete a task that they would not be able to do independently, with the intention of gradually increasing their pupil's skill set and confidence.

Examples of scaffolding often refer to pupils' use of language and writing, for example, providing word banks to help pre-teach vocabulary. In addition to modelling, other scaffolds which can be used to assist pupils making art are often practical. Providing assistance with materials will help a pupil to produce an outcome which they would otherwise struggle to make. Here are a few examples:

- pencil grips
- rulers with grips
- water pots with non-spill lids
- self-threading needles
- thick thread for sewing (e.g. wool)
- shape templates
- a pre-drawn space (e.g. square or rectangle) for a pupil to draw in
- pre-rolled/cut clay
- pre-cut cardboard/paper.

Practical scaffolds might be appropriate for individual pupils (for example, a pencil grip for a Year 1 child who struggles to grip their pencil to be able to complete a line drawing with appropriate pressure). They can also be used with an entire class where natural manual dexterity at a particular age necessitates extra assistance (for example, self-threading needles combined with thick thread for Year 2 who would struggle to thread a conventional needle with thin cotton).

A small number of pupils may be assisted by adapting the materials they use for a particular task, where the standard materials impose a barrier to learning. Let's look at a case study which illustrates this.

Case study: Adapting tasks for every learner to thrive

In Year 5, pupils in Miss Salisbury's class are studying Islamic design. They have learned that Islamic designs often contain repeated geometric patterns built on combinations of repeated squares and circles, which may be overlapped, to form symmetrical and intricate forms.

The pupils draw their own symmetrical pattern, inspired by Islamic design, using a compass and a ruler. They paint inside the small shapes they have created with three different hues of brightly coloured inks using a small brush.

David, in Miss Salisbury's class, struggles to control a pencil whilst drawing. When he uses a small brush, painting inside small shapes, he finds it difficult to pull the brush in a controlled way. If he sees that he is not succeeding in a task he quickly becomes upset and may use the brush in a destructive way.

Miss Salisbury adapts the task slightly for David. He will create a symmetrical pattern, using the same materials but on a slightly larger scale. Instead of drawing a circle with a compass he draws around a template. He creates straight lines using a ruler with a grip. He uses a medium-sized brush to paint inside large shapes he has created.

Note how the theoretical, disciplinary and practical content of what David has been taught is the same as everyone else in the class. The curriculum remains ambitious for all of the pupils, including David.

For further information about inclusive teaching in the art classroom see Chapter 3.

Providing feedback

The Ofsted research review (2023) highlights the importance of pupils having 'timely, frequent and bite size' feedback to make progress when performing practical tasks in art.

What does this mean for teachers in the classroom? Giving pupils time to make art should be a part of every art lesson. During this time teachers can be actively engaged in a dialogue with individual pupils to guide their practice. This 'timely and frequent' interaction ensures that teachers are addressing what pupils are doing as they do it. This is much more effective than commenting on work after a lesson has finished. It ensures that pupils can address a teacher's comments in the moment, as they work. It also allows teachers to address pupil's misconceptions as they come up.

Feedback is most useful to pupils if it is specific, broken down into manageable steps and linked to key ideas which they have been taught during the course of the lesson. This can include making links between practical, theoretical and disciplinary knowledge. Eisner (1988) explores the value of making these connections to 'illuminate the relationships between concepts, skills and generalisations'. By engaging in a dialogue with a pupil as they work, a teacher can encourage them to recall what they have learned, make connections and improve their practical skills.

As subject leads we can ensure that teachers in the classroom are aware of the importance of immediate feedback by making this the focus of lesson observations and professional development sessions.

In practice: providing verbal feedback in lessons

Here is an example of how teachers/other adults in the classroom can actively engage in dialogue with pupils as they work. During the course of a unit, pupils in Year 4 have been learning that variations of tone made by cross-hatching can indicate where light falls on an object and make a drawn object look three-dimensional or 'real'. This combines practical, theoretical and disciplinary knowledge. Their key learning point is that cross-hatching looks dark when lines are close together and lighter when lines are further apart. They are asked to draw a still life object from observation.

Here is a series of questions which an adult in the class can ask to encourage pupils to recall what they have learned, make connections and improve on their cross-hatching skills:

- Look at the still life objects. Where is the lightest highlight/darkest shade on the objects you are looking at? Why are some parts light or dark?
- Do the objects in your drawing look three dimensional? Why? Why not?
- How have you shown different tones in your drawing? Show me a highlight/shade on your drawing.
- What makes cross-hatching look dark/light? How can you make the shades darker/highlights lighter in your drawing?

Chapter summary

- Teachers often lack confidence in their own artistic skills which can be a barrier to effective teaching. As subject leads we can find practical ways to address this.
- Teachers need to explicitly instruct pupils to use materials by modelling.

- Modelling is a scaffold where teachers provide information in specific, manageable steps to allow pupils to learn a particular technique or skill.
- To encourage divergent outcomes or creative experimentation teachers can model a range of possibilities to act as a starting point for a child's imagination.
- Other scaffolds relevant to making art are often practical.
- It is important that pupils receive feedback as they work to guide their practice in art.

Questions for reflection

- Which artistic skills are teachers in your school confident about teaching? Which skills do they lack confidence teaching? What different strategies can you put into place to improve confidence?
- Is modelling part of every lesson? Is it specified in lesson plans?
- What is the quality of modelling? What strategies can you put into place to improve modelling?
- What practical scaffolds do teachers use? Are necessary resources available?
- Do teachers give feedback as pupils work in art lessons? How does their questioning elicit and build on children's knowledge and skills?

Explore further

- Rosenshine's 'Principles of Instruction: Research based strategies that all teachers should know'
- Eisner's, 'Structure and magic in discipline-based art education'

8 Practice and the importance of process

A good art education in a primary school offers pupils a rich blend of learning about the language of art and the opportunity to practise creating art. Creating art involves developing skills using a variety of media and learning the different processes to create art.

This chapter discusses the processes which pupils will go through when creating art. It explores how, as subject leads, we can ensure that pupils develop their application of these different processes. It considers how undertaking such processes allows pupils to develop their own creativity, self-expression and identity.

This chapter looks at:

- the meaning and importance of process in art
- exploration and experimentation
- invention, design and planning
- evaluation
- the importance of drawing
- using sketchbooks.

Process in art: meaning and importance

A process is a series of actions or steps taken to achieve a particular end. In the creation of art we undertake many different processes. The current National Curriculum for England (DfE, 2013) uses a variety of words to pinpoint some of the processes which are used in the creation of art: explore, experiment, think critically/analyse, invent, design, develop, share and record ideas, create/make and evaluate.

Part of the process of creating art is using different media to make objects. The skills which pupils should develop in the making process are discussed in Chapters 3, 4 and 9. Many people will think that the development and perfection of such skills is all there is to making art. Whilst important, concentrating solely on developing these skills will not fully explore the creative possibilities and potential for self-expression which art as a subject offers.

There are many ways to define processes, other than the practice and development of skills, used in the creation of making art. We can distil these to:

- looking (see Chapter 6)
- analysing (see Chapter 6)
- exploring/experimenting
- inventing
- designing/planning
- evaluating.

Process, in the study of and creation of art, is important. We should actively reflect on its importance because we naturally tend to prioritise outcomes or results over how those results are achieved. From an early age pupils can be highly critical of artwork they produce. For almost all people who practise art into adulthood this persists. Educational structures such as measuring progress by exams and increasing use of artificial intelligence serve to emphasise this tendency. By using artificial intelligence and asking a machine to produce an instant result eradicates the thinking, researching or writing process we would otherwise go through and stunts the development of those capabilities.

A more constructive attitude is to value the *processes* involved in creating art whether or not those processes result in an outcome that pleases or displeases the maker. Failures can be as useful as successes for the developing artist who is willing to ask 'why did that not work?' The repetition of the same or similar processes will help the pupil develop both physical artistic skills and artistic perception.

In the subject of art, part of pupils' growing knowledge will relate to process: knowledge of *how* to look, analyse, explore, invent, design and evaluate. We should teach pupils the value of these processes. They connect our body with our senses, brain and spirit and allow us to use art as a vehicle of self-expression.

Exploration and experimentation

Exploration and experimentation are key processes in the study of art. Pupils explore ideas, feelings and what they see through experimentation with different materials. These processes require imagination and can be a vehicle for self-expression.

Creativity has been described as the 'capacity to imagine, conceive, express, or make something that was not there before' (NACCCE, 1999). Exploration and experimentation are part of such creativity and may, or may not, result in an outcome which we perceive to be 'finished' (or even be pleased with). Exploration and experimentation can be described as 'visual thinking'. Lack of what we perceive as an outcome, for example, a finished painting, does not devalue the process of exploration and experimentation. It is valuable in itself.

Some maintain that the very nature of the freedom which exploration and experimentation imply means that it cannot be taught but only facilitated by providing opportunities to explore and experiment. Providing such opportunity has been described as providing an 'emergent space' (Briggs, 2025).

Whether or not we think such exploration and experimentation can be taught or facilitated, as art leaders we need to consider practically how the curriculum provides this and what it can look like in the classroom. How do we integrate it into the practice of art in our schools?

How do we integrate exploration and experimentation into classroom practice?

One way of exploring is by looking. The importance and value of looking is discussed in Chapter 6. As described in Chapter 6, the process of exploration by looking can be integrated into every art lesson. Let's look at some other ways of integrating exploration and experimentation into classroom practice.

Material literacy and exploration/experimentation

Another way of exploring in art is by experimenting with different materials. Making progress in art is in part about learning how to use materials with increasing facility. This has been referred to as 'material literacy' (Briggs, 2025). Of course, part of achieving material literacy will be to follow established techniques with a variety of materials. Some such techniques are described in Chapter 9. A pupil without skills to manage a particular material will find it difficult to fulfil their expressive intentions (Eisner, 1997). This does not mean that learning and practising such skills and techniques should preclude creative exploration. Learning technical skills should be balanced with an exploratory approach.

Chapter 1 discusses how the Ofsted Research Review implies a rather linear approach to providing a balanced curriculum where skills are learned first and then creativity comes afterwards (Ofsted, 2023). This of course is one approach. For example, a pupil can be taught how to shade with a pencil by observing a simple three-dimensional object in front of them. They can then embark on a freer task, such as putting objects together in a surrealist manner, where they use the shading technique they have learned.

Practice in the classroom, however, reveals that creative development and the development of particular skills and techniques do not always occur in such a linear way but can occur concurrently. All artistic output can involve some element of the imagination. Take, for example, drawing a daffodil from observation. This may at first appear to be a task which involves little personal expression, however, it still involves considerable individual creative input in how the pupil creates colour and tone (Robinson, 1995).

Convergent and divergent outcomes

The Ofsted research review (Ofsted, 2023) addresses the need for balance between pupils learning established skills and using their own creative exploration by reference to knowledge which is acquired to achieve certain outcomes. Convergent outcomes are where 'we are aware of how pupils will apply this information [knowledge] for example, specific techniques to command a particular skill'. Divergent outcomes are 'where we do not know how pupils will use the knowledge pupils draw on the knowledge to create their own artwork, combining what they know in sometimes experimental contexts for example, the use of different media or visual cues can convey a personal style'. Let's see how divergent outcomes can be facilitated in the classroom.

Providing stimulation for the imagination

Tasks which allow pupils to take a freer approach, experiment with ideas, materials and produce divergent outcomes should be balanced with tasks which produce convergent outcomes. This allows pupils to explore and take risks. Most pupils, however, will find this hard to do if they are given nothing to fuel their creativity. Teachers need to provide stimulation for the imagination.

This stimulation will often be most fruitful if pupils encounter it in the context of a series of lessons and it is connected to what they are learning about. Exploration and experimentation, rooted in subject-specific knowledge, will produce a wide array of personal, expressive responses from different pupils.

In practice: exploration and experimentation tasks within art lessons

The following table sets out some examples of tasks which use exploration and experimentation in response to particular artists, genres, methods and concepts. Providing such tasks in each key stage allow pupils to connect theoretical, practical and disciplinary knowledge with their own creative and imaginative initiatives.

Key stage	Context	Artists/examples	Activity
Lower/upper Key Stage 2	Abstract expressionists - conveying emotion in abstract works	Jackson Pollock Alma Thomas	Listen to a piece of music that pupils work from to produce an abstract painting that reflects their own emotional response to the music.
Upper Key Stage 2	Photography - photomontages	John Stezaker David Hockney	Pupils produce their own photomontages which juxtapose contrasting images from magazines.
Lower Key Stage 2	Lines - an artists' basic tool	See Figure 8.1	Experiment using lines to draw a feather from observation using a variety of different media (for example, pen, charcoal, wax resist with ink wash).
Lower Key Stage 2	Negative space (the space between objects)	Rene Margitte's *Decalcomania* (1966, Centre Pompidou, Paris)	Cover paper with charcoal and use a rubber to draw the negative space observed in a pile of twigs.
Key Stage 1	Symmetry in art	Leonardo da Vinci's *The Last Supper* (1495–1498, Santa Maria delle Grazie, Milan)	Create symmetrical sculptures using plastic objects found in the classroom.
EYFS	Painting inside shapes using primary colours	Miro's *Figures and Dog in Front of the Sun* (1949, Kunstmuseum, Basel)	Draw imaginary people using wax crayons. Paint inside the shapes made using watercolours in primary colours.

Figure 8.1 Year 6 drawings of a feather from observation using a variety of different media

In practice: exploration/experimentation outside art lessons

Exploration and experimentation does not have to be confined to art lessons, although integrating it into art lessons is important to ensure that an explorative/experimental approach is not missed from the curriculum. Teachers can also be encouraged to provide opportunities for exploration/experimentation with different materials outside art lessons. Opportunities might include:

- Where pupils have a 'soft start' or an opportunity in breakfast/after school club, providing quick, independent drawing exercise.
- Providing a variety of materials for pupils to use on different tables in the classroom on a rotating basis, every day, ten minutes before lunch break.
- Where pupils finish a task in another lesson early, ask them to create a ten-minute drawing/painting/sculpture from observation or from the imagination.

- **Providing pupils with a variety of simple drawing materials to use during break times.**

Invention, design and planning

The process of creating a piece of art needs invention. The very act of creation is personal and expressive, rooted in individual personality and character. The National Curriculum (DfE, 2013) reflects this: pupils are expected to 'explor[e] their ideas and record… their experiences'. The importance of generating ideas is reflected as one of three strands alongside making and evaluation, in NSEAD's Key Stage 1 and 2 curriculum framework (NSEAD, 2014).

The process of invention can also involve other processes, for example, looking, analysis, exploration, experimentation and evaluation. It necessitates using the imagination. Pupils can use the work of other artists to inspire their own imagination and invention. Over a course of lessons a pupil may:

- Look at a work of art made by another artist, answer questions and discuss it using theoretical, practical and disciplinary knowledge and a variety of subject specific vocabulary.
- Use the work as inspiration to explore and experiment with a particular idea, material or technique.
- Invent/create their own work using that idea, material or technique.
- Evaluate their own work and the work of their peers in the light of their growing theoretical, practical and disciplinary knowledge.

The methods which artists use to invent or create vary. Some may work intuitively, as with artists who use a method called 'automatism', such as Jackson Pollock. Pollock is thought not to have planned his paintings but have created them 'in the moment', dripping large amounts of household paint onto a horizontal painting surface placed on the floor.

Other artists might plan or design what they want their artwork to look like by making preparatory drawings. Some painters, such as J.M.W. Turner, are known for sketching outside and then using their sketches to make a more detailed, scaled-up finished painting inside. Some sculptors, such as Henry Moore, are known for creating small 'maquettes' (small, experimental, three-dimensional models) which they then scale up to create a larger, finished sculpture.

Introducing pupils to the different ways that artists can work is part of understanding the discipline of art. In doing so they further their disciplinary knowledge. They also do this by exploring how they, as artists themselves, can work in different ways. For subject leads this means that it is important to ensure that the curriculum allows pupils to both work intuitively (such as drawing directly from the imagination) and plan through sketching and experimenting with different materials and ideas in their sketchbook (see page 115).

Evaluation

For an artist, part of creating art is pausing, looking and assessing what they have made. This process of evaluation should be part of what pupils learn to do. For pupils, evaluating their own work in the light of their growing theoretical, practical and disciplinary knowledge informs their own creative progress.

Evaluation can take place at any point in a lesson or series of lessons but is most typically beneficial if pupils reflect on their work at the end of a lesson, at the beginning of the next lesson or at the end of a series of lessons. The last lesson in a series can be devoted to evaluating and doing further work on a piece in the light of conclusions drawn from pausing, looking and assessing. Subject leads can ensure that evaluation is not missed out by specifically timetabling it and ensuring that it is taking place when they monitor activities.

Whilst reflections can be written down by older pupils (and may appear in sketchbooks), what is more important is that all pupils get the opportunity to reflect on, evaluate and orally discuss what they have produced. This includes looking at the work of their peers and engaging in discussion about what each other has produced.

Ask pupils to engage in a 'silent gallery'. They quietly walk around looking at each other's creations and stand by a work which they want to talk about which they then discuss.

When pupils comment on the work of their peers it is important that teachers instil a culture of respect ensuring that comments are positively framed. For all artists, whatever their age, engaging with other people's views about their work is personal and exposing. Commenting with specificity is one way of ensuring a positive and effectively evaluative culture. Comments which specifically relate to pupil's growing knowledge, using subject-specific vocabulary, learned over the course of a series of lessons are not only useful but allow pupils to recall and revise key methods, concepts and ideas.

Subject leads can provide teachers with a bank of questions which provoke focused conversation in which pupils can specifically use their practical, theoretical and disciplinary knowledge to reflect on their work. Often questions which start with the word 'how' work best. Here are some examples:

- How have you used cross-hatching to show tone?
- How do the colours you have used give the illusion of light?
- How have you used lines to show space?
- How have you used your brush? What effect does this have?
- How have you used your pencil? What effect does this have?
- How does this piece reflect your identity?
- How does this piece make you feel? How is this achieved?

The importance of drawing

Drawing is a fundamental skill in the creation of art. Many artists, working in a variety of different materials, see drawing as their starting point. The artist, Maggi Hambling likens it to a musician doing their scales or a dancer doing their exercises (Hambling, 1990).

As well as being a fundamental skill, drawing can also be seen as a process. Just as other artistic processes are intrinsically valuable, so is the process of drawing. Whilst we may instinctively value drawing as an outcome or product, we also need to understand the value of it as a process.

Artist Luke Hawker reflects the value of the process of drawing and what it can teach us, with these words:

> *'To learn best, we must first realise [drawing] isn't a fixed goal to achieve, it is instead a process in itself... drawing as a process can teach us about our subjects and ourselves' (Hawker, 2025).*

The Royal Drawing School in London reflects on the intrinsic importance of drawing:

> *'We believe drawing is both an end in itself and a route to innovation and learning. It's a fundamental life-skill that allows us to understand the world around us' (Parker, 2025).*

Children use drawing to express themselves and communicate from a very young age, before they learn to read or write. There is a lack of self-consciousness in the way that they draw which many artists look at with envy.

Drawing as a mode of personal expression is a reflection of how it, as a process, connects a person's interior world with the material world around them. Drawing is the process by which there is connection between eye, brain, hand and physical material. This is why when we look at drawings, we see them as deeply personal. We instinctively recognise the individuality of the mark on the page and how that mark is reflective of the person who has made it.

Drawing is also intrinsically connected to looking. This connection also demonstrates the physicality of drawing as a process. Drawing makes us observe more closely, which in turn make us stop and connect with the material world around us. The connection between drawing and looking is discussed further in chapter 6.

There are different modes of drawing: drawing can be observational, come from the imagination, be exploratory, investigative and generative. It is often the process by which artists record and develop ideas. We might describe this process as 'visual thinking'.

As subject leads, it is important that we ensure these different modes of drawing are all reflected in our school curriculum. Developing drawing as a skill, using a variety of materials, observational drawing, and the connection between the process of drawing and looking, are discussed at other points in this book. Let's consider now what ideas and methods we can give teachers to ensure pupils experience drawing as an imaginative, exploratory, investigative and generative process.

In practice: imaginative, exploratory, investigative and generative drawing

Here are some examples of tasks/methods which can be used in the classroom through which pupils can express, explore, investigate and generate ideas. These can be used as warm-ups at the beginning of a lesson, as a task which is central to a lesson, or used outside lessons in situations such as those discussed in 'Exploration/Experimentation outside art lessons' above.

These tasks/methods can all be used with pupils of any age. If used both within and outside art lessons, teachers have the potential to ensure that drawing is a daily activity.

Task	Description
Draw four quick line drawings of a bird or other animal.	• Drawing one: from the imagination. • Drawing two: using a continuous line (once the pupils have put the pencil on the page they cannot take it off). • Drawing three: made using the pupils' non-dominant hand. • Drawing four: made with the pupil's eyes closed. • Give pupil 15 seconds to do each drawing. • See figure 8.2, for example.
Draw a variety of animals from the imagination using a limited number of shapes for each animal.	• Example one: drawing of a cow using only squares and rectangles. • Example two: drawing of a chicken using only circles and ovals. • Example three: drawing of a cat using only triangles • Use photographs of the animals as stimulation for the imagination.
Do several drawings of an object, using any drawing material, within a decreasing time frame.	• Draw for five minutes. • Then three minutes. • Then one minute. • Then 30 seconds. • Finish with ten seconds.
Draw something directly from the imagination, such as a landscape with buildings or trees.	• Only use repeated lines, i.e. no colouring or shading. • See figure 8.3, for example.
Use different grades of pencils to create different lines.	• Experiment: create different patterns just with lines. • Start with only straight lines. • Then just use curvy lines. • Experiment using two different types of pencil: 2b then 6b. • Experiment: press hard and soft with each pencil.
Draw the same object from observation using a variety of different media.	• Different media such as pen, charcoal, wax resist with ink wash. • See figure 8.1 (page 108), for example.
Experiment with drawing using mixed media.	• Draw different lines (pencil, wax, felt tip). • Cover with blocks of colour in ink or watercolour. • Create marks on top (pencil, charcoal, chalk and felt tip). • See figure 8.4, for example.
Draw using a variety of materials whilst listening to music.	• Use long pieces of paper. • Use different lines, shapes and colours to map music as it plays.
Draw close up sections of a highly textured object.	• Highly textured objects such as wood, fabric, shells and leaves. • Pupils 'zoom in' with their eyes to a small section of the object. • Draw, shapes, patterns, textures using pencils, charcoal or oil pastels.

Figure 8.2 Year 3 quick line drawings of a bird: from the imagination, using a continuous line and drawn with their eyes closed

Figure 8.3 Year 1 landscape drawn from the imagination using repeated lines

Figure 8.4 Year 6 experimental drawing using mixed media

Using sketchbooks

The current National Curriculum for England (DfE, 2013) requires that Key Stage 2 pupils are taught to 'create sketchbooks to record their observations and use them to review and revisit ideas'.

This stipulation reflects the fact that sketchbooks have been and are central to the way most artists work, and are a vital factor in understanding and creating art. They can also be used by younger children as well as those in Key Stage 2.

Many art leaders ask: How should we use sketchbooks? What should be in them?

A good starting point is to introduce teachers and pupils to the sketchbooks of famous artists. Good examples are the sketchbook of Leonardo da Vinci, Van Gogh, Turner, Frieda Kahlo and William Kentridge. In their sketchbooks these artists record what they see, draw from their imagination and develop their ideas by experimenting with a variety of different materials. Sometimes they might accompany their pictures with writing, recording their observations and thoughts. Often artists will stick images or even small objects into their sketchbooks which interest or inspire them.

Within the primary school setting sketchbooks should be reflective of a rich art education. They might include:

- exploratory, experimental and warm-up drawings/paintings using a variety of materials
- annotated reproductions of other artists' work
- objects and cuttings
- the products of research
- written reflections
- written evaluations of pupils' finished works.

Using sketchbooks should be integral to how pupils work in the classroom. They need to be explicitly shown how to use them. This should be woven into art lessons. Lessons should guide pupils in using their sketchbooks as spaces for exploratory work, including drawings, paintings, collage, exercises, experiments, cuttings, annotations and written reflection. A curriculum might include, for instance, a lesson, or series of lessons on sketchbook use at the beginning of Key Stage 2 when pupils are expected to make more and more use of them. Encourage teachers and teaching assistants to keep their own sketchbooks and to share these with the children. Pupils can also make simple sketchbooks themselves at the beginning of the year which then becomes the sketchbook which they use in forthcoming lessons. Modelling the use of sketchbooks is discussed in Chapter 9.

If sketchbooks become integral to how pupils work in art lessons, they may show the development of ideas for a particular project over a course of lessons. Or perhaps a series of stand-alone pieces developed over a course of lessons and linked by a particular theme/concept. As well as using sketchbooks during art lessons, sketchbooks can be integrated into a daily drawing routine outside art lessons. As such, a sketchbook may not have a particularly identifiable coherent order to an outsider, *but that does not matter.*

Sketchbooks are a place for collecting, researching, observing, thinking and reflecting. What a sketchbook is *not* is an ordered, pristine book. They are working, developing documents which are as likely to include material which a pupil may choose not to develop as to include material which feeds into larger, finished pieces. It is easy to fall into the trap of treating sketchbooks solely as evidence for inspections and monitoring, which exhibit 'finished' work in an orderly way. This does not fit into the definition of 'sketchbook' as most artists use them. It does not allow them to be exploratory documents, including useful failures as well as successes. As such it is appropriate that teachers' marking or annotations in pupils' sketchbooks are kept to a minimum. This is discussed further in Chapter 10.

Chapter summary

- Pupils' knowledge of process in art involves: understanding *how* to look, analyse, explore, invent, design and evaluate.
- Exploration and experimentation should be integrated into classroom practice through the use of different materials and learning how to use those materials.
- Creating a piece of art requires invention. Pupils can use the work of other artists to inspire their own imagination and invention.
- Pupils should evaluate their own work. This can be done orally or in writing. Evaluation is most effective where pupils specifically relate their own work to practical, theoretical and disciplinary knowledge.
- Drawing is a fundamental and valuable process in creating art. Different modes of drawing include: observational, imaginary, exploratory, investigative and generative. These should all be reflected in the school curriculum both within and outside art lessons.

- Sketchbooks are a place where pupils can collect, research, observe, think and reflect. They are a vital tool in the art classroom and can be used with children of all ages.

Questions for reflection

- How are exploration, experimentation, invention, planning and evaluation integrated into the school curriculum?
- What evidence of these processes do you see in the classroom/in sketchbooks?
- How is experimentation balanced with learning skills?
- What is the balance of convergent and divergent outcomes?
- Are pupils given the opportunity to work intuitively as well as planning their work?
- What drawing opportunities does the school curriculum provide within art lessons and outside art lessons?
- What are sketchbooks like?

Case study: Creating more drawing opportunities across the school

Ahmed is a subject lead and is keen to increase the opportunities for drawing amongst all year groups. He has identified that the art curriculum provides for a variety of drawing activities with different materials, but she feels that the school could raise the profile of art at school by integrating drawing more generally into school life.

He talks to SLT about where in the school day drawing opportunities could be created. They identify three options:

1. Each day there is a soft start in which pupils from Years 2–6 read. Pupils could be given the option of drawing in their sketchbooks instead.
2. Lunchtime staff have recently talked about some pupils being disruptive during playtime after lunch. The lunchtime staff think there could be some calming activities provided, which could include drawing.

3. Pupils in Key Stage 1 spend 15 minutes before lunchtime listening to a video recording of a story while children wash their hands in rotation. Two or three days a week this could be changed so that pupils are given the opportunity to draw instead.

Ahmed puts together a bank of drawing tasks with simple instructions to be presented to the pupils on a whiteboard/laminated sheets. These tasks are appropriate for all ages and can be presented directly to the pupils for each of the scenarios detailed above.

He takes 15 minutes of a staff meeting to talk to teachers/teaching assistants about how to implement the drawing tasks in scenarios one and three above, demonstrating how pupils can use the instructions and resources. He does the same with lunchtime staff in their weekly catchup meeting.

He uses subject leadership time to drop into lessons/lunchbreaks to assess how the drawing activities are going and diarises to review the project with staff/SLT after one term.

Explore further

- Paula Briggs from Access Art talks about material literacy, convergent and divergent learning, emergent space and process (art as a 'verb' rather than as a 'noun') in this video: www.accessart.org.uk/three-lenses
- The artist Maggi Hambling talks about drawing in the BBC programme 'Making Their Mark: Six Artists on Drawing' (1990): www.bbc.co.uk/iplayer/episode/p02t7k03/making-their-mark-six-artists-on-drawing-maggi-hambling
- Access Art has resources and ideas about sketchbooks, including making sketchbooks: www.accessart.org.uk/sketchbooks

9 Basic principles in drawing, painting and sculpture

This chapter looks at some of the key media and basic principles in drawing, painting and sculpting which pupils will use at primary school. These are the three major techniques which are required to be taught by the National Curriculum for England (DfE, 2013).

This is not intended to be a comprehensive guide in relation to each technique (that could be the subject of an entire book!) but seeks to offer guidance about key skills and resources which teachers will repeatedly encounter whilst teaching art in the primary setting.

Some of you may have extensive personal knowledge of the practices, skills, materials and related concepts discussed in this chapter. Others will be less confident. Whatever your position, this chapter addresses the subject knowledge your teachers will need so that you can work with them to develop their knowledge. This will ensure that your teachers are equipped to teach their pupils a variety of skills using a variety of media.

In this chapter we will cover:

- mark making
- drawing development
- painting development
- sculpting development.

The 'Explore further' section at the end of the chapter has suggestions about where you can source extra information and training in each area.

Mark making

You may have heard of the term 'mark making'. This refers to the act of making any kind of mark, with any material, whether it be by drawing, painting or making a mark into three-dimensional materials such as clay. It can mean the creation of lines, dots, patterns or textures. It is seen as fundamental for artistic expression, whether marks are spontaneous (for example, scribbling) or more considered (for example, cross-hatching or shading). It is often referred to as fundamental for young children in the first stages of exploring materials and developing fine motor skills. Its importance continues, however, all the way through primary school, and it is always an underlying consideration while children are drawing, painting or sculpting.

Developing drawing skills

The importance of drawing is discussed in Chapter 8. For an artist, drawing is akin to a musician practising their scales. It is fundamental to the creation of visual art. Many of the elements of art discussed in Chapter 3 can be explored by the process of drawing: we can create marks, lines, patterns, shapes, different tones and the illusion of light, space and texture all by drawing.

As art leaders, we should ensure that a wide variety of materials are being used in our schools to draw. These can include pencils, chalk, charcoal, crayons, soft pastels, oil pastels, felt-tip pens, biros and inks. We can provide pupils with different surfaces which provide a variety of thicknesses and textures on which to draw. These can include different weights of cartridge paper, newsprint (which is thinner and often has a smoother surface than cartridge paper), sugar paper of varying colours (this is rough and absorbent), cardboard and found paper such as magazine paper or fliers.

Combining a variety of drawing materials and surfaces (commonly called 'mixed media') can be fruitful and provide for a degree of exploration. Experimental and warm-up drawing activities are discussed in Chapter 8.

Different ways to use lines

One way to draw is by using lines. Lines are like an artist's basic tool. The German artist and theorist Paul Klee (1879–1940) talked about how important lines were to him: he is said to have commented that 'a line is a dot that went for a walk' and 'drawing is simply a line going for a walk'.

Let's think about the fundamental nature of lines as a tool in visual art. From lines pupils can create shapes and patterns. Certain types of line have names (straight, curved, zigzag) and such lines can be used to create shapes. Some of these shapes have names (circle, square, rectangle). We call these geometric shapes. Pupils can also use lines to create organic shapes (which are shapes which we cannot name). Organic shapes are often found in nature, for example, the outline of a leaf or a stone.

Pupils can use lines in an intuitive way, to express themselves, to create something from their imagination and as a tool to try to represent reality. They can use a whole variety of materials to draw lines (for instance graphite and charcoal). They can also 'draw' imaginary lines with their fingers in the air or create lines in space using materials like string or metal.

Creating visual texture with mark making

Sometimes, drawing is referred to as mark making. Van Gogh used a variety of different marks using ink to create the illusion of texture (how something physically feels) in his drawing *Street in Saintes-Maries-de-la-Mer* (1888, The Metropolitan Museum of Modern Art, New York). Pupils can use this as inspiration and use a variety of drawn marks to show texture. Ask pupils to carefully observe a natural object close up and create different marks in charcoal (dots, dashes, longer lines and squiggles) to represent what they see (see Figure 9.1).

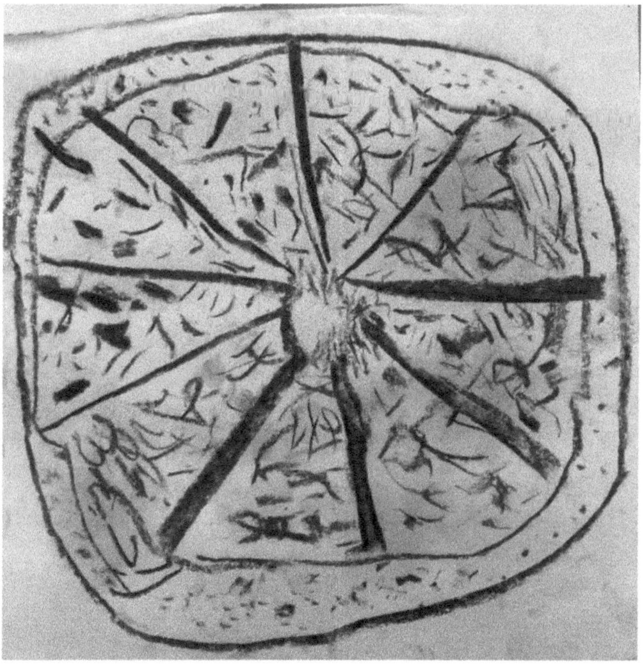

Figure 9.1 Year 2 charcoal drawing of an orange showing texture through mark making

Different ways to create tone with a pencil

Tone means how light or dark something is. Varying tone shown on a drawn object can create the illusion of three-dimensional form. A drawn apple will appear spherical if part of it is lighter (a highlight), part is darker (shade) and other parts show tones in between these two extremes (mid-tones).

There are different ways in which artists create tone by drawing in monochrome. Using repeated lines, whether in one direction or by cross-hatching with a pencil is an effective way to create tone. The closer the lines are together and the greater the line weight (for example, by pressing harder with a pencil) the darker an area will be. This is shown in Rembrandt's *Self-Portrait in a Cap* (1630, Rijksmuseum, Amsterdam). When learning these techniques, at first pupils have a tendency to create rigid lines, which look as if they have been drawn with a ruler. Encourage them to be freer by holding their pencil with a less tight grip. See Chapter 6 for an example of a Year 3, cross-hatched still life (Figure 6.3).

Another way of creating variation in tone is by using a pencil to shade. Shading is where we create very small marks with the pencil so that it almost impossible to distinguish the marks from each other, giving the impression of a block of shaded tone. Shading can be made darker or lighter by pressing harder or more softly with the pencil. Pupils sometimes make their marks too long whilst shading which has the effect of showing defined marks (giving a scribbly effect) rather than giving the appearance of a block of shade. Encouraging pupils to create small marks will ensure that this doesn't happen. See Figure 9.2 for an example from a Year 6 pupil of a shaded ear inspired by the anatomical drawings of Leonardo da Vinci. Note here how the pupil has left the highlights unshaded, using the white of the paper in to indicate light.

The weight of a line or darkness/lightness of an area of shading can be accentuated by introducing pupils to different grades of pencil. The softness of the graphite is indicated by the H/B scale. The higher the H number the harder a pencil will be and the higher the B number the softer the pencil will be. Using a soft 6B pencil will allow pupils to achieve dark shading or heavy, bold lines. For lighter or more delicate and precise lines an HB pencil (the mid-point between the H and B scales) could be more appropriate.

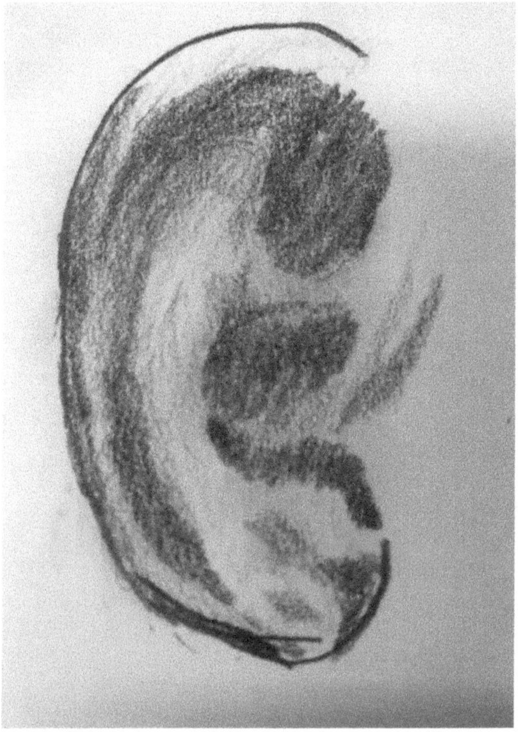

Figure 9.2 Year 6 shaded ear using a pencil

Chalk, charcoal, blending and negative space

Pupils often enjoy using chalk and charcoal because it provides a bolder way of creating lines and tone than using graphite. It can also be successfully smudged, blended or rubbed away with a finger or a rubber to create subtle variations in tone or line. Using charcoal to show dark shades and chalk to show highlights whilst working on coloured sugar paper can produce an effective gradation of tone and illusion of form. See Figure 9.3 for an example of a Year 3 chalk/charcoal pear drawing from observation. Note how the presence of the dark cast shadow creates an effective three-dimensional feeling. Blending can be used in a similar way with soft pastels (as opposed to oil pastels) to create coloured forms.

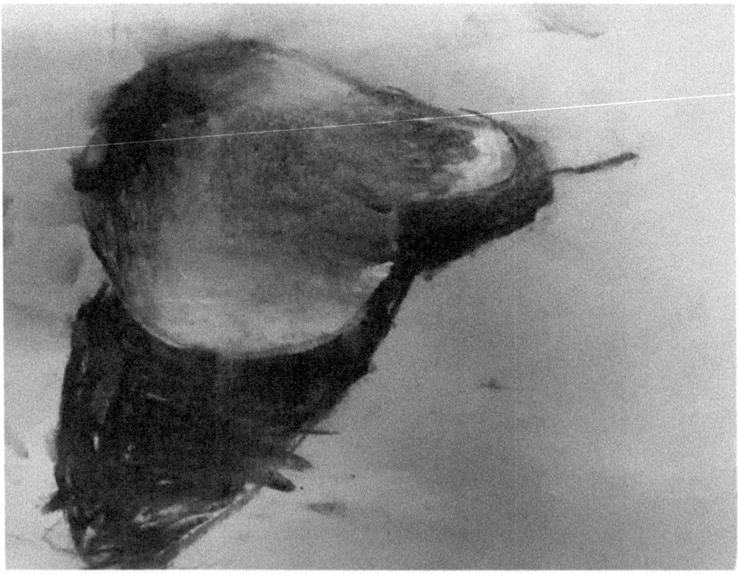

Figure 9.3 Year 3 chalk and charcoal pear on coloured sugar paper

Using charcoal with a rubber is also a good technique to explore the concept of negative space. This means the space around and between objects. Ask pupils to draw a group of natural objects, such as a pile of twigs or leaves. At first, get them to cover a piece of paper with charcoal using the side of the stick. Then, ask them to rub out negative shapes between the objects they can see using a rubber. They will be left with the shapes of the twigs or leaves.

Drawing with ink

We can use various different tools to dip into ink and draw, including conventional dipping pens, feathers, brushes and even sticks. Tools which provide an unpredictable thickness of line can create expressive, fluid drawings. Because ink cannot be rubbed away it is a perfect medium for creating a developing sense of freedom: pupils have to dispense with their desire for each of their marks to be 'perfect' and work with what appears on the page. Conventional handwriting pens are also useful, particularly when paired with water and a brush so that pupils can drag the still-wet ink across the page to add tonal values. See Figure 9.4 for a Year 6 drawing using this method.

Figure 9.4 Year 6 ink drawing

Working with oil pastels: dark to light

Oil pastels (different from soft pastels) are a particularly useful drawing medium in the primary classroom. They can provide bright, bold colours and are successful when worked on coloured sugar paper and combined with other media. They are not mixed by rubbing them with a finger, as with soft pastels, but by layering colours on top of each other so that the oil content of the two colours blend.

Oil pastels are an opaque material and as such are conventionally worked with by layering colours on top of each other, starting with dark colours, working towards lighter colours.

Developing painting skills

Using different tools with which to paint and using different varieties of paint can provide exciting expressive opportunities for pupils. Many of the elements of art discussed in Chapter 3, such as colour and texture, can be explored by the process of painting. Painting is good for exploring colour mixing and colour theory.

Painting materials

Pupils can experiment using different kinds and consistencies of paint. Poster paint is a very affordable option. It comes ready mixed or can be mixed from a powder with water. It can be mixed with PVA glue, sand and different amounts of water to change its consistency. It is easy to clean from clothes, brushes and hands, dries quickly and gives bold results. It often shows up brushstrokes clearly where pigment collects in certain areas so isn't appropriate for a smooth finish.

Acrylics, which come in tubes and are also fast-drying, whilst more expensive, provide richer colours. They can also be applied to almost any painting surface, so are a good investment.

Watercolour paints come in two forms, solid 'pans' (small blocks) and tubes. Pans are easier to use with pupils and come in variety of qualities. More expensive types provide richer colours. All these paints are mixed with water to dilute them.

It is important to carefully think about the surface pupils will paint onto. Cartridge paper, of the thicker variety, multimedia paper and watercolour paper all hold paint mixed with water well. These papers will have different surface textures (from smooth to bumpy) which will affect the finish. Thinner types of paper will tear apart if a lot of water is added with the paint, which is often the case with watercolours. For watercolour it is often advisable to use very thick cartridge paper or special watercolour paper (although this is often expensive). Acrylic paint works effectively on canvas and cardboard.

Different types of brushes are appropriate for different types of paint. Traditionally hog's hair (or imitation hog's hair) brushes, which have rougher bristles, are used for acrylics. Sable (or imitation sable) brushes, which are much softer, are used for watercolour. Brushes come in different sizes and shapes (for example, flat or round head). What size and shape the pupils use will depend on what kind of brushstrokes they wish to make. Choosing the right brush (for example, a small round brush to paint small, fine brushstrokes) should be part of what pupils are expected to learn.

A whole variety of other tools can be used for applying paint. Sponges are good for covering a whole area or producing a stippled effect, particularly on a big scale. Sticks or toothbrushes can provide pupils with an unpredictability and a freedom of application.

Colour mixing and using a brush

From primary colours (red, blue and yellow) children should learn how to mix secondary colours (orange, green and purple) and tints and shades (where white is added to make a colour lighter and where black is added to make a colour darker). They can mix all three primary colours to create brown. They can also try mixing tertiary colours and exploring complementary colours or analogous colours. Complementary colours are pairs of colours which are opposite each other on the colour wheel (purple and yellow, orange and blue, green and red) which when placed next to each other create a strong visual contrast. Analogous colours are colours which are next to each other on the colour wheel and create a serene effect when used together. Both complementary colours and analogous colours are a useful tool to demonstrate to pupils how colour can affect our emotions. A good example is Munch's use of orange and blue next to each other in *The Scream* (1893, National Museum, Oslo) which, combined with swirling lines, create an unsettled feeling.

When they are very young, pupils should be given the opportunity to experiment mixing different colours together, discussing the results. As they get older, pupils should be explicitly taught how to mix colours effectively and hold/use a brush. Mixing effectively means mixing colours thoroughly in a mixing palette, washing the brush each time before loading it with different colours and getting an appropriate ratio of water to paint on the brush. A common technique when mixing two colours is to blend from 'light to dark'. This means starting with the lighter colour and adding very small amounts of the darker colour until the desired colour is reached.

A brush can be held in different ways depending on the type of brushstroke that a pupil wants to achieve. A delicate, precise brushstroke will require holding the brush in a similar controlled way that a pupil would hold a pencil, using the 'tripod' grip at the point where the metal of the brush meets the wood. If pupils want to use freer brushstrokes they may choose to experiment with how they can do this with an appropriate brush.

Pupils can consciously learn that using the brush in different ways will create a variety of brushstrokes. To create a smooth effect they should ensure that the brush is loaded with a reasonable amount of paint that is not too dry or lumpy and pull the brush (rather than push it so that the hairs become splayed). Pupils can experiment with getting different ratios of water to paint on the brush which will change the density of the colour. To create a stippled effect, to suggest texture, the brush should be drier and used more vertically in a dabbing motion so that the finished effect shows the individual hair marks.

Painting with acrylics: dark to light

As long as they are not diluted too much with water, acrylic paints will appear opaque. In a similar way to other opaque materials (such as oil pastels mentioned above) these are conventionally treated by layering colours on top of each other to produce a depth of colour, starting with the darkest tones and working towards the lightest.

An extended still life project (for example, painting colourful forms such as fruit and vegetables) is a good way to explore using acrylics to work from dark to light. Pupils can start by using a technique established by the 'old masters' (a name conventionally given to expert painters in Europe between the thirteenth- and seventeeth-centuries) where a ground (a wash which covers the entire page) in a light brown (e.g. yellow ochre) covers an initial sketch. The darkest tones on the objects are then painted in a mid-brown (e.g. burned sienna). This is then painted over in layers using the colours the pupil wants to paint the objects (e.g. tones of green/yellow for an apple) working from dark to light. Between each layer, when working with this technique, it is necessary to allow the paint to dry.

Painting with watercolours: light to dark

Watercolours, as their name suggests, are used by adding lots of water to the pigment. By adding more water to a colour the tone will get lighter as the pigment becomes more dilute. It is therefore often advisable with watercolours to add water to a colour to make it whiter, rather than white.

There are two basic ways of working with watercolours. The first, called 'wet-on-wet', is where an initial colour is applied to the paper and another colour is added while the first colour is still wet. This creates an effect where one colour bleeds into another. This creates an unpredictable effect which can be good for when pupils want to experiment or use a free approach. The second, called 'wet-on-dry', is where the second layer of paint is applied to an area of paint that is already dry. In this instance the colours do not bleed but rest on the paper in layers which produce a darker colour which is a combination of both of the colours.

If working 'wet-on-dry', as with acrylics, watercolour paints can be layered on top of each other to produce a depth of colour. However, because watercolours are translucent, they are conventionally layered with the lightest colour first, working towards the darkest colours last (light to dark).

Watercolours are particularly successful if used to make large areas of thin washes. Pupils might like to work on top of these with mixed media or apply a wash to something already drawn with pencil or a water-resistant material such as a wax crayon. First, pupils should make a wash, which means some paint with a lot of water in a puddle in their palette. A wash can be applied to wet or dry paper (i.e. wet-on-wet or wet-on-dry). Pupils will probably find it easier to apply the wash to wet paper as this often gives a more even finish. So, first wet the paper with water using a large brush. Then, once the paper is wet apply the wash evenly over the page. Avoid brushing over the paint again and again as this will wear out the paper.

In practice: working with watercolours

The bullet points below present a task which children in either Key Stage 1 or Key Stage 2 can complete to experience working with watercolours using the wet-on-wet, wet-on-dry and light to dark techniques. For this task use watercolour paints in pans, imitation sable brushes and watercolour paper.

1. **First, ask the pupils to experiment painting wet-on-wet to see the different effects they can get.**
   - **With a large imitation sable brush, paint a circle of colour.**
   - **While the circle it is still wet add a different colour paint, allowing it to bleed into the other colour.**
   - **Experiment with painting lots of different circles using different combinations of colour and different amounts of water.**

2. **Do a similar task painting wet-on-dry.**
   - **This time, using a large brush paint circles in light colours and leave the circles of colour to dry.**

- Then, using a smaller brush and darker colours paint over the circles with different lines, shapes and patterns.
- Observe how the wet-on-dry effect is different from the wet-on-wet effect.

3. Combine these effects to create a small abstract painting inspired by plants in different shades of greens, yellows and reds using circles of colour, lines and patterns (see Figure 9.5, for example).

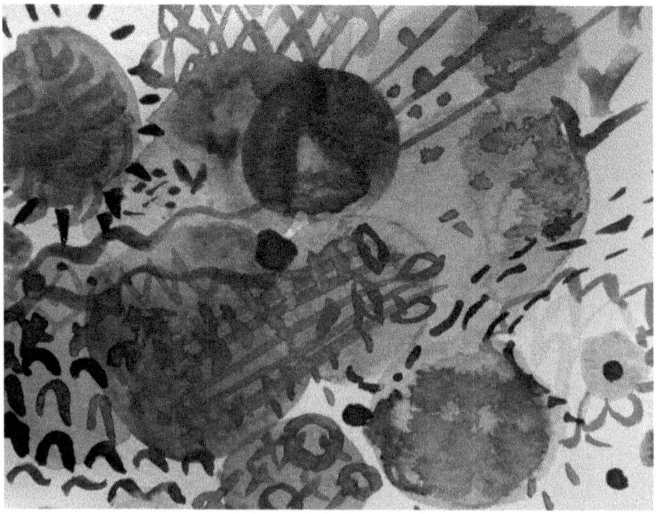

Figure 9.5 Year 6 abstract watercolour painting using wet-on-wet and wet-on-dry

Developing sculpting skills

Sculpture is an area which many teachers will feel unsure about teaching, largely because of the messiness of and unfamiliarity with the materials. It is, however, a very important part of visual art particularly because many children, who may struggle with skills such as writing and drawing which require developed fine motor skills, thrive when working with materials in three dimensions. The tactile nature of sculpture materials also often provides a freedom for children with special educational needs.

Sculpture is artwork which has three dimensions. It is important to define this with pupils and find age-appropriate language to do so, particularly with young children. I would sometimes refer to sculpture as 'art which you can touch all the way around'.

Many of the elements of art discussed in Chapter 3 can be explored by the process of sculpting such as form, space and scale. It is important for children to experience sculpture first hand, rather than just photographs of sculpture, to understand its three-dimensional quality. This can be by accessing statues/sculptures in local public spaces (which are often on a large scale) or showing children smaller scale work which can be brought into the classroom.

Sculpture can be made by building materials up or carving materials away. There are many materials from which we can make sculpture: clay, plaster, wax, metal such as bronze or steel, stone, paper, cardboard, found natural objects, recycled objects and many more. Materials which children can experience in the primary classroom include dough (such as homemade salt dough), clay, card/paper, found natural/recycled objects and wire.

Working with clay

As most primary schools do not have a kiln the obvious choice of clay is air-dried clay which hardens and holds its form once dried without the necessity for firing. Air-dried clay is readily available and relatively cheap. A type of clay called 'new clay' can be used if pupils want to work on something over a number of days or weeks. This clay can be moistened and stored in a plastic bag to keep it workable over time. Once left to dry, it will behave in the same way as air-dried clay and harden.

Basic equipment for dealing with clay are boards to work and roll clay on, small rolling pins, wooden rolling battens (which act as a guide for thickness when rolling) and plastic clay tools for cutting/drawing into the clay.

Pupils should be encouraged to be experimental when working with clay, however there are some basic techniques that they can learn which will ensure that their work is solid and sound. When joining any bits of clay together pupils should score the edges which will be joined and then apply slip to them (a mixture of water and clay) before joining and smoothing the join with their fingers. This will ensure that the clay sticks soundly together once the clay has dried. They should avoid adding parts to any work which are too thin and long as these will be weak and liable to break once dry.

Pots, containers and cylinders can be made by using coils, flattened coils or slabs. The simplest form of pots, suitable for very young children are 'thumb pots', where pupils create a ball and push their thumbs into the centre to create a cavity. As well as building clay up pupils can create texture/patterns by using tools to create marks in the clay or by pressing textured material such as fabric into the clay. Clay can also be painted to create sculptures in colour. The best paints for intensity of colour are acrylics. These can be covered with PVA glue or Mod Podge which creates a shiny, varnished finish.

Case study: Bringing sculpture into the classroom

Juan discovers through learning walks, lesson observations and talking to teachers and children that, despite various different sculpture projects being provided for in the school curriculum, these aren't taking place. He would like to ensure that each year group is undertaking at least one sculpture project a year to ensure that pupils are learning about and making sculpture as this is a requirement of the National Curriculum.

He talks to three teachers from different key stages to determine why this is not happening. He finds out that the teachers don't understand how to use the materials they are supposed to be using and that they find the mess the pupils make when using them challenging. This means they avoid teaching the lessons. He also discovers that the Year 3 teacher, Fatima, has knowledge and skills working in clay from an evening class which they attended and is keen to share their expertise.

Juan identifies the skills and activities which are supposed to be being taught in each year group. He changes the materials used in each activity so that they are more limited: either clay or cardboard. He asks Fatima to run a staff training session on working with clay so the teachers get hands on experience and increase their confidence about what they need to teach.

Juan suggests the sculpture lessons are all taught after lunch break so that a member of staff, with the help of some older children, can set up the resources for each class. He reorders the timetable so that classes doing sculpture without a sink can swap with another class with a sink. He ensures that his subject leadership time over the course of a half-term is timetabled to enable him to monitor the sculpture lessons.

Example PD session: working with clay

Here is an example of what a PD session on improving teachers' knowledge of working with clay might look like.

<table>
<tr><th>TIMING SUGGESTION</th><th>SESSION GUIDANCE</th></tr>
<tr><td>5 mins</td><td>Discuss the importance/relevance of teaching clay skills, the wider curriculum links and the benefits this will have to their understanding of sculpture and creating art.</td></tr>
<tr><td>10 mins</td><td>With a fist-sized lump of air-dried clay, a wooden board, a rolling pin, a plastic cutting tool, a pot of water and an extra small pot demonstrate how to make a coil pot. Explain that this will cover some basic principles of working with clay. It is designed to build teacher's knowledge about working with clay and will allow them to demonstrate some basic techniques to their classes with increased confidence.

• Take one-third of the lump of clay and squash it into a ball. If it is too hard work water into it so that it is malleable.
• Squash the ball with the heal of your hand against the wooden board. Roll it out using the wooden battens as a guide to thickness.
• Using a circular object as a guide, cut out a circle with the plastic tool. Make sure the circle isn't stuck to the wooden board. This is the base of your pot.
• Score around the edge of the circle with the tool.
• Take a lump of clay and roll a long 'worm' which is approximately 0.5 cm thick. Make sure you don't roll it too much so it cracks and becomes brittle.
• Make some slip by mixing a little clay and water in a pot. With your finger, put the slip around the scored edge of the base.
• Place your coil around the base on top of the slip. Smooth the join between the base and the coil on the outside and the inside.
• Keep adding coils so that your pot grows. Each time you put clay on top of clay remember to score, apply slip and smooth down.</td></tr>
<tr><td>25 mins</td><td>• Allow time for each person to make their own coil pot.
• All teachers should review what they have learned by making the pot. They should write down three pieces of advice which they would pass on to another person completing the task.
• Ask each teacher to do this activity with their class at some point during the next week while the activity is still fresh in their mind, making use of their three pieces of advice. This will be a good opportunity for them to practise their modelling skills.
• Ask each teacher to think of another activity using clay which uses the same techniques they can do with their class during the course of the next term.</td></tr>
</table>

Chapter summary

- The teachers on your team need knowledge of different practices to be able to teach them successfully.
- Drawing is a fundamental skill for creating visual art. As a subject lead, provide a variety of drawing materials to explore different practices.
- Different drawing practices include exploring different ways of using lines, using marks to create texture, exploring ways of creating tone with a pencil, using chalk, charcoal, ink and oil pastels.
- Painting gives pupils the opportunity to explore different materials and concepts (e.g. colour and texture). Teach different techniques such as colour-mixing, how to use a brush, painting dark to light with acrylics and painting wet-on-wet, wet-on-dry and light to dark with watercolours.
- Making sculpture is an opportunity for children to engage in a tactile way with three-dimensional form. A variety of sculpture materials such as clay, card/paper, found natural/recycled objects, and wire can be used in the primary classroom.

Questions for reflection

- What drawing, painting and sculpture opportunities presently exist in your school?
- What materials does the school presently use?
- What new drawing, painting, sculpture opportunities/materials could you use in your curriculum?
- What knowledge do the teachers have of working with these materials?
- Do you have any experts amongst your staff?
- What kind of training could you find/provide?

Explore further

- Access Art provides activities and professional development opportunities in drawing, painting and sculpture: www.accessart.org.uk

- NSEAD (National Society in Education for Art and Design) offer bespoke training for teachers: www.nsead.org/courses-advice/professional-development-courses/bespoke-training
- Various national museums have resources and workshops in-person and online: www.royalacademy.org.uk/teachers-and-schools, www.nationalgallery.org.uk/learning/teachers-cpd-sessions and www.tate.org.uk/schools
- Resources/workshops offered by galleries/museums/artists local to your school

Drawing

- *Drawing is a Class Act: A Skills-Based Approach to Drawing,* book series by Meg Fabian
- *Thinking and Learning Through Drawing: In Primary Classrooms* by Gill Hope

Painting

- *Painting is a Class Act: A Skills-Based Approach to Painting,* book series by Meg Fabian

Sculpture

- *Make, Build, Create: Sculpture Projects for Children* by Paula Briggs
- *Art Shaped: 50 sustainable art projects to kickstart children's creativity* (2023) by Darrell Wakelam

10 Assessment, monitoring and implementing change

Assessing what pupils know and understand, what they can do and whether they are making progress is a key part of being a teacher (Wyse et al., 2022). As subject leads we need to ensure that the teachers in our schools understand how to assess children's progress. We can then monitor how effectively art and design is being taught and what implications this has for change.

What is assessment? It has been described as observing and interpreting what pupils do and say and using this information to judge how learning can be improved (Assessment Reform Group, 2022).

We need assessment to be purposeful. Charts and tick-boxes which map individual pupil progress are not effective and needlessly add to teacher workload if the information gathered is not used to implement change. Purposeful assessment provides information which enables teachers and subject leads to consider what adjustments need to be made to what is taught and how it is taught.

Assessment is often seen as a difficult and contentious area in art and design (Fleming, 2012). Qualitative evaluation in a subject which involves subjectivity seems almost like trying to square a circle. There are often no 'right' answers in art as we might encounter in maths or science. The Ofsted research review (2023) makes clear that this is a difficult area stating that 'issues of subjectivity can challenge both the validity and reliability of assessment practices'. It is important, therefore, to be clear about what we are assessing and how we do it. To guide you in this, this chapter looks at:

- what are we assessing?
- formative assessment
- summative assessment
- uncovering impact: how do we identify what children know?
- marking sketchbooks
- making use of our findings
- monitoring and implementing change.

What are we assessing?

Before considering how to assess, it is important to consider what progress teachers should be assessing. Being clear about what we are assessing means understanding, in the first place, what it is we want pupils to learn. Michael Fordham summarises it like this:

> *'A curriculum sets out the journey that someone needs to go on to get better at the subject... it* models *the progress that we would hope (although cannot guarantee) that someone will make. The curriculum* is *the progression model.' (2020)*

A good art curriculum should allow pupils to learn practical, theoretical and disciplinary knowledge and make connections between these three areas. This means knowing, understanding *and* learning how to do things and building on knowledge and skills year on year.

To be able to assess what we expect pupils to learn, it is essential for teachers to have a clear understanding of what is in the curriculum they use and how it builds and progresses. This will allow teachers to see what knowledge and skills pupils start with and whether this is what we expect; gauge where there are gaps and misconceptions; and understand if pupils are making expected progress.

For a teacher to have such an understanding it is helpful to summarise the key practical, theoretical and disciplinary knowledge that pupils are expected to learn and undertake during the course of a unit. This can be used as a benchmark to understand progress. This will help a teacher to assess what progress pupils should make during the course of a unit and over the course of a year. If they also have the equivalent information in relation to what pupils have done in a previous year, this helps a teacher to know what knowledge and skills they should expect a pupil to start with.

Case study: Year 1 unit on colour and the key learning points

Here is a summary of the key learning points from a Year 1 unit on colour in the art and design curriculum used by the Knowledge Schools' Trust. Teachers in the Trust have this information for each unit they teach.

Theoretical	Practical	Disciplinary
• Mondrian – *Composition with Red, Yellow and Blue* (1930, Kunsthaus, Zurich): primary colours • Van Gogh – *Sunflowers* (1888, National Gallery, London): warm/cool colours, primary/secondary colours • Hockney – *A Bigger Splash* (1967, Tate Britain, London): tints and shades to show water • Monet – *The Sea at Fecamp* (1881, Staatsgalerie, Stuttgart): contrasting brushstrokes for the sea and sky	• Holding a brush like a pencil to give good control. • Controlling the amount of water/paint that is loaded onto the brush. • Washing the brush before loading it with a new colour. • Mixing secondary colours, tints and shades thoroughly in a mixing palette. • Pulling the brush smoothly, painting inside a shape. • Experimenting with a brush to create different brushstrokes. • Experimental mark making in pencil and wax. • Looking at/analysing other artists' work. • Exploring/experimenting. • Inventing. • Evaluating.	• Colour can be used to convey different moods and effects. • Mark making with different materials can be used to convey different moods and effects. • Artists can use a variety of media to create pictures.

Formative assessment

Formative assessment provides a teacher with feedback about what pupils know, understand or what they can do, so that they can adapt their teaching if necessary. The teachers' assessment informs their teaching in the moment, which in turn informs pupils about what they can do to improve (Ofsted, 2023).

Formative assessment is sometimes known as assessment *for* learning or assessment *as* learning. It has been described as 'central to classroom practice' and is 'the process of seeking and interpreting evidence for use by learners and their teachers to decide where the learners are in their learning, where they need to go and how best to get there' (Assessment Reform Group, 2022). Dialogue is seen as central to formative assessment (Ofsted, 2023 and Assessment Reform Group, 2022). It is a dynamic process which takes place in a lesson.

What does formative assessment look like in an art and design lesson? There are a variety of ways that a teacher may assess or understand what a pupil knows, understands and what they can do during an art lesson. This can include:

- listening to pupils' responses to questions and discussions
- observing pupils as they produce written work, for example, annotations or written evaluations in a sketchbook
- observing pupils as they are engaged in the practical activity of making art.

It is important as subject leads to ensure that teachers are aware of the key learning points in a lesson/unit so this can guide formative assessment during a lesson. When a teacher has a clear understanding of the key learning points, whether these relate to practical, theoretical or disciplinary knowledge, they can advise a pupil where they need to improve, and address misconceptions and gaps in knowledge.

Formative assessment is most effective if it takes place in a timely way, when pupils are talking or working. It should be clear, specific, constructive and allow pupils to put advice into action during the course of the lesson (Assessment Reform Group, 2022). It should be 'timely, frequent and bite-size' (Ofsted, 2023).

In practice: examples of formative assessment

Formative assessment can usually be witnessed in a classroom as a dialogue between teacher and pupil. Here are some examples of formative assessment 'in action':

- **Clarifying meaning where a pupil demonstrates a misunderstanding about subject specific vocabulary (for example, 'visual texture' means when an artist uses different shapes, marks, colours, light and shade to show how something feels).**
- **Clarifying conceptual misconceptions (for example, a sculpture can be made from a variety of three-dimensional materials, rather than just clay).**
- **Addressing gaps in knowledge (for example, explaining that Cézanne is a 'post-Impressionist' artist).**

- Giving feedback to pupils about how they can improve techniques when engaged in practical activity (for example, explaining and demonstrating how to mix colours thoroughly in a palette before applying them to a page).
- Discussing ideas and how these can be implemented using a particular material (for example, discussing the use of colour theory to understand the effect of the use of certain colours in an abstract painted work).

Summative assessment

Summative assessment is when teachers assess whether pupils have learned, over time, what the curriculum sets out for them to learn.

As we have seen, an art and design curriculum should set out how a pupil's practical, theoretical and disciplinary knowledge builds. If pupils follow the curriculum their knowledge should build. Summative assessment means judging whether this is happening.

It is tempting to think that summative assessment is just about using a 'final' piece of work at the end of a unit to assess whether a pupil has learned what we expect. In maths or science, where the 'final' piece of work might be an exam, this seems relatively simple. This is not so in art. Assessing a 'final' piece of work in art (such as a finished drawing, painting or sculpture) is seen as problematic because of the subjective nature of aesthetic judgement (Ofsted, 2023).

Not only does the subjective nature of aesthetic appreciation mean that assessing a final piece can be difficult, but a final piece will exhibit a complex combination of factors which demonstrate progress in knowledge, understanding and skills which a pupil has learned across the curriculum (Ofsted, 2023). Unravelling this demands a clear understanding from the teacher about what pupils are expected to have learned over the course of a series of lessons and how these are demonstrated in a final piece. Let's explore how we could approach this with a practical example.

In practice: assessing a final piece

In the Year 1 unit on colour, discussed in the case study above, having looked at and discussed Monet's *The Sea at Fecamp* (1881, Staatsgalerie, Stuttgart) pupils in the class each spend a lesson producing a painting of a stormy sea. Figure 10.1 shows a painting produced by one of the pupils. The teacher has summarised the practical knowledge which the unit covers using simple bullet points, in the manner of the case study on page 138. They are therefore able to see at a glance that the painting shown in Figure 10.1 demonstrates a grasp of the following practical knowledge:

- Holding a brush like a pencil to give good control.
- Controlling the amount of water/paint that is loaded onto the brush.
- Washing the brush before loading it with a new colour.
- Mixing tints and shades thoroughly in a mixing palette.
- Pulling the brush smoothly.
- Experimenting with a brush to create different brushstrokes.

They are also able to determine, upon discussion with the pupil when they are evaluating their work at the end of the lesson, that they understand the theoretical and disciplinary knowledge that:

- Monet used contrasting brushstrokes for the sea and sky in *The Sea at Fecamp*.
- Colour and mark making can be used to convey different moods and effects.

Figure 10.1 Year 1 painting of a stormy sea

Uncovering impact: how do we identify what children know?

As well as assessing a final piece, it is also important to understand that we can assess in different ways, using a variety of tools. Using such a variety of tools helps teachers and subject leads form a more comprehensive view of progress. The following table explores some of these tools and how they can be used for both formative and summative assessment. It is a matter of judgement and agreement with senior leaders, with an eye to teacher workload, what summative assessment activities teachers are expected to undertake and with what regularity. Note that the Ofsted research review says that 'it is important that summative assessments take place at sufficiently long intervals to allow time for enough curriculum content to be taught and learned' (2023).

Method (description and use)	Formative assessment	Summative assessment
Questioning and conversations		

• Different methods of questioning can provoke answers and conversations which reveal knowledge and understanding as well as misconceptions and gaps in knowledge.
• These methods can be used to identify knowledge of vocabulary, processes/techniques, art/artists as well as more complex disciplinary knowledge such as how art is valued and why.
	• This is an important feature of every part of an art lesson to assess and guide pupils' learning.
	• It's particularly important during:
	  • prior learning
	  • looking/ analysing
	  • as pupils work/ practise
	  • plenary.
		• Questions and conversations can be used to gauge pupils' understanding at the end of a unit when they engage in:
		  • evaluation of their own work/work of their peers
		  • during pupil voice (see 'In practice – questions for pupil voice').

<table>
<tr><td colspan="3">Looking at sketchbooks</td></tr>
<tr>
<td>• Work in sketchbooks such as drawings, annotations and notes can show evidence of the use of different processes:
◦ looking/analysing
◦ exploration/experimentation
◦ invention/design/planning
◦ evaluation.
• Drawings/paintings in sketchbooks can show evidence of developing practical techniques using a variety of materials.</td>
<td>• Look at sketchbooks as pupils' work can be used to assess and guide their learning as they work.</td>
<td>• Looking at sketchbooks at the end of a unit can be used to gauge pupils' understanding at a fixed point in time.</td>
</tr>
<tr><td colspan="3">Using knowledge organisers</td></tr>
<tr>
<td>• Techniques such as blocking out information from a knowledge organiser can be used as a tool for assessment to embed knowledge such as:
◦ vocabulary and definitions
◦ identification of art and artists
◦ practical knowledge such as definitions of colours found in a colour wheel.</td>
<td>• Organisers used during the course of a lesson can reveal understanding and address misconceptions and gaps in knowledge.
• They are particularly useful when asking pupils to retrieve knowledge during:
◦ prior learning
◦ plenary.</td>
<td>• They can be used to gauge pupils' understanding at the end of a unit when they engage in:
◦ evaluation of their own work/work of their peers
◦ during pupil voice (see 'In practice – questions for pupil voice).</td>
</tr>
<tr><td colspan="3">Using multiple-choice quizzing</td></tr>
<tr>
<td>• Multiple-choice quizzing can be used to isolate knowledge such as:
◦ vocabulary and definitions
◦ identification of art and artists
◦ practical knowledge such as definitions of colours found in a colour wheel.</td>
<td>• Isolated multiple-choice questions can be used when asking pupils to retrieve knowledge during:
◦ prior learning
◦ plenary/ review.</td>
<td>• Groups of questions can be used to gauge pupils' understanding at the end of a unit in tandem with evaluation of their own work/ work of their peers.</td>
</tr>
</table>

Marking sketchbooks

Sketchbooks (more fully discussed in Chapter 8) are a place for collecting, researching, observing, thinking and reflecting. They are pupils' working, developing documents. It is easy to fall into the trap of treating sketchbooks solely as evidence for inspections and monitoring, which exhibit 'finished' work in an orderly way. This does not fit into the definition of a 'sketchbook' as most artists use them. It does not allow them to be exploratory documents.

As such it is appropriate that teachers' marking or annotations in pupils' sketchbooks are kept to a minimum (Gregory et al, 2020). Not only does this approach ensure that sketchbooks are kept as exploratory documents, but it acknowledges that the most effective feedback (particularly when pupils are engaged in practical activity) happens in dialogue between teacher and pupil at the time a task is being completed. It also minimises teacher workload.

It is of course helpful for pupils to receive affirmative comments about their work, and seeing this in written form can reinforce those comments. It may also be helpful for pupils undertaking projects which span a series of weeks (more likely in Key Stage 2) for individual next steps to be summarised in writing. In both cases, comments made on sticky notes, rather than directly on the page of a sketchbook, are effective. This ensures the integrity of the exploratory nature of the sketchbook is kept intact.

Finally, affirmative comments about a pupil's work are an ideal opportunity for a teacher to reinforce key knowledge and skills which a unit has sought to teach. For example, rather than saying, 'fantastic drawing skills!' a comment might read, 'fantastic drawing skills – you have effectively shown different tones with the variety of your cross-hatching'.

Making use of our findings

It is clear that teachers need to use their findings from formative assessment to adapt their teaching, as they teach to help pupils improve. This means addressing gaps in knowledge and misconceptions as they arise.

What do teachers/subject leads do with the information gathered as a result of summative assessment? What are the implications when we discover that there are gaps and misconceptions in knowledge and skills?

There are various actions a teacher can take if, as a result of assessment, they find an individual, group or whole class have developed misconceptions or have gaps in their knowledge. These can include:

- Pre-teaching vocabulary, concepts or investigating pieces of art/artists in advance of a lesson.
- Re-teaching during subsequent lessons where there are gaps in knowledge and misconceptions.
- Giving more time during subsequent lessons for looking at/investigating a particular image.
- Giving more time during subsequent lessons for opportunities to practise.

As subject leads we should also ask teachers to share findings as a result of assessment with us. This is part of subject monitoring and helps us to consider whether amendments or adjustments need to be made to the curriculum or if there are pedagogical considerations which require attention.

Monitoring and implementing change

Subject monitoring is wider than, but connected to assessment. As subject leads we need to review the implementation of the art curriculum. This means having systems in place which monitor pupils' overall progress and also evaluate the effectiveness of the curriculum. We need to ensure that appropriate modifications are implemented as a result of monitoring.

We can think of the process of monitoring as gathering evidence, reviewing and improving. Here are some suggested ways of gathering evidence to assess effective implementation:

- reviewing planning
- observing lessons
- undertaking informal learning walks
- looking at sketchbooks
- undertaking pupil voice (this can include looking at and discussing sketchbooks, outcomes and/or knowledge organisers with pupils)
- asking teachers for feedback about curriculum/implementation/key findings from assessment (this could be done by way of a questionnaire).

To get a clear picture about progress, subject leads may want to undertake these activities two or three times during the academic year with a broad range of selected pupils and teachers.

As subject leads we then need to reflect on our findings, discuss these with the senior leadership team and give feedback to teachers. A spirit of collaboration is important here, where feedback engages with successes as much as areas for improvement. Any action points which arise as a result of monitoring can be incorporated into a subject development plan (discussed in Chapter 1).

Action points which arise out of monitoring are likely to fall broadly into two categories:

- Training and supporting staff.
- Reviewing and amending the curriculum.

Training and supporting staff might entail:

- Discussing/agreeing class timetables with SLT/teachers to ensure there is sufficient curriculum time for each unit.
- Identifying successes and giving clear, achievable targets which arise out of lesson observations.
- Providing opportunities for peer-on-peer lesson observations.
- Working with teachers in individual year groups to clarify key learning points for each unit.
- Providing PD sessions during staff meeting time on areas pinpointed for development (e.g. practical subject knowledge/practice; modelling/scaffolding in art; questioning methods to aid the process of looking; assessment in art – setting expectations).
- Ensuring appropriate resources are available for each unit.

Amendments/adjustments made to the curriculum might include:

- Providing more opportunity to practice a particular skill.
- Adjusting curriculum sequencing so that teaching of a particular skill happens in a more appropriate order and is broken down into manageable steps.
- Adjusting theoretical/disciplinary content so that concepts are more age-appropriate.
- Providing more opportunity to work with a particular medium.

- Providing more opportunity for processes such as exploration, planning and evaluation.

In practice: questions for pupil voice, looking at sketchbooks and lesson observations

Pupil voice, looking at sketchbooks and lesson observations are all key activities involved in monitoring. Here are example questions you can use for each one. Questions for pupil voice (to include looking at and discussing sketchbooks, outcomes and knowledge organisers):

1. What can you tell me about the Renaissance?
2. How did you explore the Renaissance in the artwork you created?
3. What skills did you develop?
4. What do you like about the artwork which you made? What would you do differently next time?
5. What do you know about different artists?
6. What do you think you can learn by looking at work by other artists?
7. What is the most fascinating thing you have learned in art?
8. Why is learning about art important?

Questions to consider when looking at sketchbooks:

1. Is the curriculum being followed?
2. What practical skills/techniques have been developed? What materials have been used?
3. What different processes can you see evidence of (looking, analysing, exploring/experimenting, designing/planning/inventing and evaluation)?
4. What theoretical/disciplinary concepts have been explored?

Questions to consider when observing lessons:

1. What prior learning is needed for pupils to access today's lesson?
2. What subject-specific vocabulary is being used in the lesson?
3. What misconceptions were made and addressed in the lesson?
4. What concepts are being built upon?

5. What practical/theoretical/disciplinary knowledge is being taught?
6. How has the teacher broken down the learning into manageable chunks?
7. How does the teacher manage behaviour?
8. What opportunities were there for pupils to share their ideas?
9. How does the teacher ensure all pupils can access the lesson?

Chapter summary

- Assessment is observing what learners say and do and then making judgements about how learning can be improved.
- To be able to assess it is important for teachers to have a clear understanding of what is in the curriculum and how it builds and progresses.
- Formative assessment provides a teacher with feedback about what pupils know, understand or what they can do, so that they can adapt their teaching in the moment.
- Summative assessment is when teachers assess, at a particular moment in time, whether pupils have learned, what the curriculum sets out for them to learn.
- We can use different tools to assess what a pupil knows and can do. This can include looking at final outcomes, sketchbooks, listening to their responses to questions and conversations and using knowledge organisers and multiple-choice questions.
- Subject leads need to monitor and review the implementation of the curriculum.
- Appropriate, realistic and timetabled modifications to curriculum content, teaching and training should be implemented as a result of assessment and monitoring.

Questions for reflection

- Do teachers in your school understand formative assessment in art and design?

- What activities are teachers expected to undertake in summative assessment for art and design in your school and how often? Is this manageable in terms of workload?
- What priorities have arisen from your recent subject monitoring? How does this affect your subject development plan?

Explore further

- 'Assessment for learning: 10 principles' by the Assessment Reform Group
- Micheal Fordham's blog: 'What did I mean by 'the curriculum is the progression model?'
- 'Assessment' in Ofsted's 'Research review series: art and design'

Bibliography

Addison, N., Burgess L., Steers J. and Trowell J. (2010), *Understanding art education: engaging reflexively with practice*. London: Taylor and Francis.

APPG (All-Party Parliamentary Group for Art, Craft and Design in Education) (2023), 'Art Now: An Inquiry into the State of Art and Design teaching in Early Years Foundation Stage, Primary and Secondary Education', *NSEAD*.

Arnold, M. (1869), *Culture and Anarchy: An Essay in Political and Social Criticism*. London: Macmillan.

Art-K (2025), 'Creative crisis: teachers report drop in fine motor skills', https://www.art-k.co.uk/art-education-neglected.

Art UK (no date), 'Visual Literacy', https://artuk.org/discover/art-terms/visual-literacy.

Assessment Reform Group, (2002), 'Assessment for learning: 10 principles', https://www.researchgate.net/publication/271849158_Assessment_for_Learning_10_Principles_Research-based_principles_to_guide_classroom_practice_Assessment_for_Learning.

Bacon, S and Tambling, P. (2023), 'The Arts in Schools: Foundations for the Future', *A New Direction, on behalf of the Calouste Gulbenkian* Foundation, https://www.anewdirection.org.uk/the-arts-in-schools.

Baddeley, A.D. and Hitch, D. (1974), 'Working Memory'. *Psychology of Learning and Motivation*, 8: 47–89.

Barnes, R. (2015), *Teaching Art to Young Children* (3rd edition). London; New York: Routledge.

Bartlett, F. C. (1932), *Remembering: A study in experimental and social psychology.* Cambridge: Cambridge University Press.

BBC (1990), 'Making Their Mark: Six Artists on Drawing – Maggi Hambling', https://www.bbc.co.uk/iplayer/episode/p02t7k03/making-their-mark-six-artists-on-drawing-maggi-hambling.

Beale, J. (2020) 'Tom Sherrington's division of Rosenshine's principles of instruction into strands'. *The Tony Little Centre, Innovation and Research in Learning* https://cirl.etoncollege.com/tom-sherringtons-division-of-rosenshines-principles-of-instruction-into-strands/.

Boaler, J. (2009). *The Elephant in the Classroom.* London: Souvenir Press.

Briggs, P. (2025), 'Thought Piece: Three Lenses', *Access Art,* https://www.accessart.org.uk/three-lenses/.

Brown P., Roediger H. and McDaniel M. (2014), Make it stick: *The science of successful learning*. Cambridge: Harvard University Press.

Burns, R. (2018), 'Applying the 'powerful knowledge' principle to curriculum development in disadvantaged contexts', *Impact,* 4 https://my.chartered.

college/impact_article/applying-the-powerful-knowledge-principle-to-curriculum-development-in-disadvantaged-contexts/.
Burns, T., and Sinfield, S. (2016). *Essential Study Skills: The Complete Guide to Success at University* (4th edition). London: SAGE.
Cooper, B. (2018), 'Primary Colours: The decline of arts education in primary schools and how it can be reversed', *The Fabian Society*, https://fabians.org.uk/wp-content/uploads/2019/01/FS-Primary-Colours-Report-WEB-FINAL.pdf.
Counsell, C. (2018), 'Senior Curriculum Leadership 1: The indirect manifestation of knowledge: (A) curriculum as narrative'. *The Dignity of the Thing*, https://thedignityofthethingblog.wordpress.com/2018/04/07/senior-curriculum-leadership-1-the-indirect-manifestation-of-knowledge-a-curriculum-as-narrative/.
Counsell, C. (2018a), 'Taking curriculum seriously', *Impact*, 4 https://my.chartered.college/impact_article/taking-curriculum-seriously/.
Counsell, C. (2024), 'What a National Curriculum can and can't do', *Schools Week*, https://schoolsweek.co.uk/what-a-national-curriculum-can-and-cannot-do/.
Cowan, N. (2010) 'The Magical Mystery Four: How is Working Memory Capacity Limited, and Why?' *Current Directions in Psychological Science*, 19(1): 51–57.
Cultural Learning Alliance (CLA) (2024), '2024 Report Card', https://www.culturallearningalliance.org.uk/wp-content/uploads/2024/05/CLA-2024-Annual-Report-Card.pdf.
Cultural Learning Alliance (CLA) (2025), '2025 Report Card', https://www.culturallearningalliance.org.uk/wp-content/uploads/2025/03/CLA-2025-Report-Card_AW.pdf.
Department for Education (DfE) (2025), 'Curriculum and Assessment Review, Building a world class curriculum for all: Final Report' https://assets.publishing.service.gov.uk/media/690b96bbc22e4ed8b051854d/Curriculum_and_Assessment_Review_final_report_-_Building_a_world-class_curriculum_for_all.pdf.
Department for Education (DfE) (2025a), 'Early Years Foundation Stage Statutory Framework', https://assets.publishing.service.gov.uk/media/68c024cb8c6d992f23edd79c/Early_years_foundation_stage_statutory_framework_-_for_group_and_school-based_providers.pdf.pdf.
Department for Education (DfE) (2013), 'National Curriculum in England: art and design programmes of study', https://www.gov.uk/government/publications/national-curriculum-in-england-art-and-design-programmes-of-study.
Department for Education (DfE) (2011), 'Teachers' Standards' https://assets.publishing.service.gov.uk/media/61b73d6c8fa8f50384489c9a/Teachers__Standards_Dec_2021.pdf
Didau, D. (2025), 'Should the curriculum be a mirror or a window', *David Didau*, https://daviddidau.substack.com/p/should-the-curriculum-be-a-mirror.
Didau, D. (2025a) 'The "Just tell them" trap'. *David Didau*, https://daviddidau.substack.com/p/the-just-tell-them-trap.

Education Endowment Foundation (EEF) (2021), *Cognitive Science Approaches in the Classroom: A Review of the Evidence.* London: Education Endowment Foundation.

Education Endowment Foundation (EEF) (2024), *Using Research Evidence: A Concise Guide.* London: Education Endowment Foundation.

Eisner, E. (1997), *Educating Artistic Vision.* New York: Macmillan.

Eisner, E. (1988), 'Structure and magic in discipline-based art education', *Journal of Art and Design Education*, 7(2): 185–196.

Fleming, M. (2012), *The arts in education*. London: Routledge.

Fordham, M. (2020), 'What did I mean by 'the curriculum is the progression model'?' https://clioetcetera.com/2020/02/08/what-did-i-mean-by-the-curriculum-is-the-progression-model/.

Gast, G. (2026), 'The essential tension between art and design', *AD Magazine,* 45 (1): 16–17.

Green, B. (2021), 'Revisiting the conceptual domain', *International Journal of Art & Design Education*, 40 (2): 436–448.

Gregory, P., March, C. and Tutchell, S. (2020), *Mastering primary art and design.* London: Bloomsbury Academic.

Hart, B. and Risley, T. (2003) 'The Early Catastrophe – The 30 Million Word Gap by Age 3'. *American Educator*, 27: 4–9.

Hauser and Wirth (2025), Frank Bowling, *Hauser and Wirth,* https://www.hauserwirth.com/artists/30000-frank-bowling/.

Hawker, L. A. (2025), Instagram @lukeadamhawker.

Howard, K. and Hill, C. (2020), *Symbiosis: the curriculum and the classroom.* London: John Catt.

Kirschner, P.A. Sweller, J. and Clark, R.E. (2006), 'Why Minimal Guidance During Instruction Does Not Work: An analysis of the Failure of Constructivist, Discovery, Problem-Based Experiential, and Inquiry-Based Teaching'. *Educational Psychologist,* 41:2, 75–86.

Leach, S. (2025) Interview with Harry Parker, *A D Magazine, 43.*

Leonard, K. (2024), 'Visual Literacy: The Missing Pillar of Primary Education', Teaching Times, https://www.teachingtimes.com/visual-literacy-the-missing-pillar-of-primary-education/.

National Advisory Committee on Creative, Cultural Education (NACCCE) (1999), 'All our futures: Creativity, culture & education', *Department for Education, and Employment, Department for Culture, Media and Sport,* https://sirkenrobinson.com/pdf/allourfutures.pdf.

Neuman, S. B., Kaefer, T., Pinkham, A. (2014), 'Building background knowledge', *The Reading Teacher*, 68 (2): 145–148.

Newmark, B. (no date), 'The secret of great curriculum design in secondary school', https://www.teachwire.net/news/the-secret-of-great-curriculum-design-in-secondary-school/.

NSEAD (2014), 'A Framework for Progression, Planning for Learning, Assessment, Recording and Reporting Generating ideas', https://www.nsead.org/files/8608849141653ba98fcb20e1e196289e.pdf.

NSEAD (2019), 'Curriculum Resources. The National Curriculum in England. Art and Design', https://www.nsead.org/static/index.html.

NSEAD (2023), 'Unpacking the Ofsted research review for art and design: NSEAD response and takeaways', https://www.nsead.org/files/9f1311767d7a5252766fe2a266f1e78e.pdf.

Ofsted (2019), 'Education Inspection Framework' (EIF), https://www.gov.uk/government/publications/education-inspection-framework.

Ofsted (2023), 'Research review series: art and design', https://www.gov.uk/government/publications/research-review-series-art-and-design.

Oftsed (2025), 'State-funded school inspection framework' https://assets.publishing.service.gov.uk/media/690b26c69456634d9795fde0/Schools_inspection_toolkit.pdf

Oxford University Press (2018) 'Why Closing The Word Gap Matters', https://www.education.ox.ac.uk/news/why-closing-the-word-gap-matters-new-research-finds-evidence-of-a-significant-word-gap-in-uk-schools/.

Patterson, F. (2011), *Photography and the Art of Seeing: A Visual Perception Workshop for Film and Digital Photography* (4th edition). Richmond Hill, ON: Firefly Books.

Primary Knowledge Curriculum (2025), 'Art Overview', https://www.primaryknowledgecurriculum.org/teacher-resources/art.

Robinson, G. (1995), *Sketchbook: Explore and Store*. London: Hodder.

Rosenshine, B. (2012), 'Principles of Instruction: Research based strategies that all teachers should know'. *American Educator*, 36(1): 12–19.

Sweller, J. (2012), 'Cognitive Load Theory' in Seel, N.M. (ed) *Encyclopaedia of the Sciences of Learning*. Boston: Springer.

Thompson, P. and Maloy, L. (2022), 'The benefits of art, craft and design education in schools: A rapid evidence review', *NSEAD*, https://www.nsead.org/files/6f85ab8587bc53ce653702da1cc15690.pdf.

Wiliam, D. (2025), 'Knowledge-rich curricula: A key driver of equity in education' in *The value of a knowledge-rich curriculum: An essay collection*. London: Civitas, pp 11–17.

Willingham, D. T. (2009), 'Why Don't Students Like School?' *American Educator*, 33(1): 4–13.

Wyse, P.D., Bradbury, P.A. and Trollope, R. (2022), 'Assessment for Children's Learning: A new future for primary education', *ICAPE*, https://www.icape.org.uk/reports-and-research/reports/2/view.

Young, M., Lambert, D., Roberts, C., & Roberts, M. (2014), *Knowledge and the Future School: Curriculum and Social Justice*. London: Bloomsbury Academic.

Index